An Encounter with Reggio Emilia

The documentation of young children's learning plays a vital role in the pre-schools of Reggio Emilia. This leading edge approach to bringing record-keeping and assessment into the heart of young children's learning is envied and emulated by educators around the world.

The fully revised second edition of *An Encounter with Reggio Emilia* is based upon a documentary approach to children's learning successfully implemented by Stirling Council in Scotland, whose pre-school educators experienced dramatic improvements in their understanding of young children, how they learn and the potential unleashed in successfully engaging families in the learning process.

This approach, which is based on careful listening to children and observation of their interests and concerns, centres around recording and commentating on children's learning through photos, wall displays, videos and a variety of different media. The authors include chapters on:

- why early years educators should use documentation as a means to enhance young children's learning;
- the values, principles and theories that underlie the 'Reggio' approach;
- how to implement documentations into any early years setting, with real-life case studies and hints for avoiding common pitfalls;
- how to involve, inspire and enthuse families and the wider community.

This text is an important read for any individual working with young children or interested in using 'The Reggio Inspired Approach' in their early years settings.

Linda Kinney was formerly Head of Learning and Development and Assistant Chief Executive of Stirling Council, UK.

Pat Wharton is an early years consultant working across several local authorities in Scotland.

An Encounter with Reggio Emilia

Children and adults in transformation

Second edition

Linda Kinney and Pat Wharton

 Routledge
Taylor & Francis Group

LONDON AND NEW YORK

Second edition published 2015
by Routledge
2 Park Square, Milton Park, Abingdon, Oxon OX14 4RN

and by Routledge
711 Third Avenue, New York, NY 10017

Routledge is an imprint of the Taylor & Francis Group, an informa business

First edition published by Routledge 2008

British Library Cataloguing in Publication Data
A catalogue record for this book is available from the British Library

Library of Congress Cataloging in Publication Data
Kinney, Linda, 1956–
    An encounter with Reggio Emilia: children and adults in
    transformation/Linda Kinney and Pat Wharton. – Second edition.
    pages cm
    ISBN 978-1-138-80896-6 (hardback) – ISBN 978-1-138-80897-3 (pbk.) –
    ISBN 978-1-315-75030-9 (e-book) 1. Reggio Emilia approach
    (Early childhood education) – Scotland – Stirling (County)
    2. Observation (Educational method) I. Wharton, Pat. II. Title.
    LB1029.R35K56 2016
    372.21 – dc23

ISBN: 978-1-138-80896-6 (hbk)
ISBN: 978-1-138-80897-3 (pbk)
ISBN: 978-1-315-75030-9 (ebk)

Typeset in Sabon and Gill Sans
by Florence Production Ltd, Stoodleigh, Devon, UK

FSC
www.fsc.org
MIX
Paper from
responsible sources
FSC® C013604   Printed and bound by CPI Group (UK) Ltd, Croydon, CR0 4YY

This book belongs to all the children, parents and families in Stirling and all the early years educators who found the courage to join us in the implementation of a documentation to early learning.

Early childhood is 'a period of momentous significance for all people growing up in our culture . . . by the time this period is over, children will have formed conceptions of themselves as social beings, as thinkers and as language users and will have reached certain important decisions about their own abilities and their worth' (Donaldson *et al.* 1983).

Contents

Preface

In reading the foreword written by Carlina Rinaldi in 2007 for the first edition we are struck by its ability to have the same resonance today as it had then. We think this because the desire to translate a Reggio-inspired approach into a Scottish context remains undiminished and our relationship with Reggio Emilia and its values and principles continue to be a source of inspiration to our thinking and practice. In the intervening years since this was written we have continued to develop our contact with Reggio Children by very regular visits and have also become members of the Reggio Emilia International Network that is global in its membership. This global identity has helped us to feel part of a community working for the common good of all children wherever a member network exists.

It is also important to make mention now, as we did then, of the help we were given subsequent to the publication of the first edition by the Bernard Van Leer Foundation, who financed us to write the modules mentioned in the Introduction and to undertake a joint project with our Reggio Emilia inspired colleagues in Amsterdam. Both these initiatives have proved to have had a significant impact on how we have continued to take forward our practice with staff teams across Stirling Council and beyond.

We continue to be honest, as the reader of these pages will hopefully know, about the joys and challenges we have faced which were identified in the foreword of the first edition. That we have continued to keep faith with the vision that we had then is a tribute to all those educators who have stood alongside us in going deeper with their understanding of pedagogical documentation and its ability to uncover the real capabilities of young children and make them visible to their families and the wider community.

We have also, during the last seven years, rejoiced in our collaboration with another local authority in Scotland who has joined us on our journey. Angus Council staff teams have worked alongside us in our quest to understand and implement pedagogical documentation into their current practice. How they have approached this with enthusiasm and energy has brought a new vitality to us since it has given us another opportunity to revisit and be thoughtful about what we think we know and what we might have to research further. Listening and engaging with the 'other' always has its possibilities for further learning.

In prefacing the foreword to the second edition we want to draw the readers attention to the original foreword to underscore how the same aspirations and vision remain. The importance of believing in these and recognising the longevity of the project cannot be underestimated. That it is a worthwhile project has never been in doubt, and we invite you encounter it within your own context, wherever in the world this is, and make a difference for your children and your families.

Foreword

Dear Reader,

This encounter with Reggio Emilia and myself had extraordinary beginnings. Pat and Linda and myself had met in Reggio Emilia and Kendal, England, and one day in spring 2002 I found myself arriving at Edinburgh Airport in Scotland being greeted by Pat. My first words were 'I don't know why I am here, but I am looking forward to finding out.' As expected, I did, since I knew that there must have been an understood and unspoken connection between the three of us which had brought us to this place. This connection was going to be significant in making a difference for children in Stirling and beyond – and so it proved to be.

What impressed me from the outset was their recognition that what they were attempting to put into practice in early years settings was an interpretation of the Reggio approach within a Scottish (United Kingdom) context; this, running counter to others who talked of 'doing Reggio'. They had understood that there could be no straight transference of this approach that did not take account of the context and culture of the country in which it was being introduced. This respect for what the Reggio approach is and can be has proved to be a cornerstone of our encounter which has allowed our contact to develop, strengthen and grow. In fact, if to educate is to develop a sense of belonging – understood as the cultural basis making it possible for each individual to find their way in their own individual story and to build a future in the dialogue with others – then the truest meaning of the Reggio approach is to help every community, every school to take responsibility for educating its children and its own future.

In this way, communities and societies will also have a new opportunity for taking responsibility for their own futures. The 'tussle' with this interpretation and its implications for the early years settings in Stirling is recorded and referred to directly throughout this book. That there have been challenges has been clearly referenced alongside the awe and wonder experienced at the amazing discoveries that educators have made not only about the children but about themselves. Making this clear to the reader will hopefully be helpful when they encounter difficulty and uncertainty in adopting this approach. The joy, excitement and challenge all fuse to make an intoxicating mix which has been captured by the authors throughout the pages of this book.

It has been my pleasure to have visited early years settings in Stirling on two visits there over the past three years, and I have witnessed the uncertainty and the struggle to understand the essence of the documentation approach to early learning and its implementation into practice. For me, I have at times been uplifted by the progress made from one visit to another, and at other times I have found myself bringing clarity to the processes of documentation when the staff had reached a 'sticking point' with aspects of it. Staff teams have been able to be honest and direct about their lack of understanding, and this was really important for me as a pedagogical consultant coming in and trying to understand their routines and practices from another European perspective.

One project that was particularly presented to me on my last visit, which is highlighted in the documentation-in-action section of this book, is the One-Eyed Rabbit. When I saw this, I was excited about it since it represented two important aspects. First, the progress that had been made by this early years setting since my last visit and second how it encapsulated many of the complexities of the documentation approach to early learning. Notably, the visibility it gave to the children's learning, which is the hallmark of this approach, along with its ability to reveal all the traces of research that the children embarked upon through their engagement with the One-Eyed Rabbit project. Others that are recorded in this chapter, though not directly seen by me, reflect a growing understanding of this approach and the generosity of the staff teams to have recorded many of their triumphs but also exposed some of their vulnerabilities and uncertainties.

In conversation with them and Pat and Linda, we have understood together that uncertainty, far from being a negative, can, without a doubt, present us with many more possibilities than certainty ever can. In the same way, what has occurred to me as significant in this project is that all the actors have come to its implementation in a collaborative mode. Admitting to each other from the outset that there was no set model to follow and, indeed, never would be, simply a set of values and principles to guide them. Researching and working out together its many possibilities and learning from each other how to take the next stage forward, this, in itself, has been an innovative departure from other projects they have embarked upon previously, and it has meant that a new fellowship has emerged between leaders, staff, children, parents and families.

What I feel it would also be important for the reader to know is that over time, each of us understood that we shared a common vision: to disseminate the documentation approach to early learning to as wide an audience as possible. To do this, we knew that we had to find a platform to realise this vision so that many more professionals could be persuaded to adopt it, thereby accessing a greater number of children to this significant way of living and working. Thanks to the funding provided and the belief in this approach by the Bernard Van Leer Foundation, the authors have been able to write this book and use it as a platform. It is clear to me that they have attempted to do this in a very straightforward way, making the journey for others hopefully less hazardous. This book marks the first stage of keeping faith with that vision.

And so our encounter and connection created in uncertainty in 2001 has realised many possibilities. Taking the risk that it could be so has been a source of both trepidation and inspiration to all those who have to date been involved in this Encounter with Reggio Emilia.

Carlina Rinaldi, President of Reggio Children
and President of The Reggio Foundation

Acknowledgements

We would like to thank all the children who have contributed to this book; the parents and families of children who have given their permission and support for their children's involvement in this book; the staff teams represented in this book; and the following early years settings: Arnprior, Croftamie, Doune, Fallin, Fintry, Raploch Nursery and Raploch Primary School.

We would also like to thank the following: Elizabeth Greig, Carlina Rinaldi, Eileen McKenzie, the Early Learning Associates team, Sharron McIntosh and the Bernard Van Leer Foundation.

What is this book about?

Like the first edition of this book, this is a very practical narrative of how we have worked with pedagogical documentation, a Reggio Emilia-inspired approach to children's learning, across most early years settings in Stirling Council in Scotland. It is our hope that it will be helpful to people across the world who are either contemplating or have started to implement it within their own cultural context.

In the first book we set out to share with the reader how we came to adopt pedagogical documentation in Stirling Council. We outlined our faltering initiation into it and where we were 6 years after its inception. It is the intention of this edition to update the reader on where we are now 8 years later in 2014. We want to do this in a way that celebrates what we have understood about children and who they really are through the implementation of this approach, while at the same time sharing ongoing and current challenges.

What is there to celebrate?

Understanding that the values had to be lived

Giving expression from the outset to the celebrations and excitements that have been generated over the last 8 years is important because experiencing these has had a motivational effect on staff teams across the Council area.

One of the most significant of these has been about the uncovering of children's innate capabilities because of the impact of working according to *the key values of pedagogical documentation* but in particular one that has been influential from the outset. This is having *an image of the child who is capable, rich in resourcefulness* and *competent in his or her own right*. We understand now that previous working practices had only given us glimpses of such capabilities. Working with such a value as one of the cornerstones of our practice we have also realised that children *need to be listened to*, be seen as people who have opinions, theories and solutions to problems, and be given the opportunity both to be listened to and heard. Each of these has also been at the heart of helping us to know our children much better and to integrate their interests, ideas and theories into our everyday practice.

Listening then, as a metaphor for having the openness and sensitivity to listen and be listened to – listening not just with our ears, but with all our senses (sight, touch, smell, taste and orientation).

(Rinaldi 2001)

Like others before us we used to think we were listening to children, but we now know that this was surface and not at the depth that really accessed us to children's thoughts, learning dispositions and creativity. Taken together, these key values have been highly influential in bringing about a paradigm shift in the thinking and practice of staff across most early years settings. This has not been to disregard the other values of this approach identified in our first book.

For example, staff have worked hard on another value – *respect* – that emphasises to children and staff the importance of working within a respect agenda as it applies child to child and adult to child and their families. Much work has been done on this particular aspect of practice with the children, encouraging them to use the language of respect and understanding what that can mean in the life of the nursery and beyond. Identifying these and core values clearly has brought with it the realisation that embedding these in practice leads inevitably to the implementation of the others. What we have clearly understood, over time, is that if these values are not firmly embedded in everyday practice this approach will not be viable and will fail to have the potential to change children's and adults' lives. Recognition of the powerfulness of their impact has been reinforced for us by visitors telling us that they get a real sense of the values being lived when they visit the settings. We celebrate this!

Learning to let children's interests lead the learning

It is true to say that, through living, one of the core values we have really learned is to listen to children's voices and as a consequence we have been able to recognise sustainable interests that individual children and groups of children may have. This has enabled us to work much more meaningfully with children and enrich their possibilities for learning. Through going deeper with our understanding of how developing children's own interests lights up their capacity to learn we have accompanied them on many exciting journeys over the past 8 years. As we have become more confident in allowing children to be the protagonists in their own learning and gradually relinquished an adult-led mode of practice we have been able to see how competent children can be as enquirers and researchers in pursuing and developing an interest that they have identified. What we have learned is that one child may ignite an interest that other children are happy to join with them in developing. Following such a philosophy, some improbable situations have occurred. For example Ben, a child in one of the rural nurseries, was persistent in his request to explore tents and camping. The Head did listen initially but once she understood how keen Ben was to research this further she consulted with the other children and the interest took off. Parents then became involved and the ultimate outcome was, after months of research, for an overnight camping adventure to be organised. Families were amazed that this should all have occurred through one child's interest. What we also now know is that all children are not demonstrating a sustainable interest all of the time; we accept this and so do the children. The depth of the learning that has emerged from such engagements with children's interests has sometimes felt overwhelming for staff, since they have often found themselves in situations where children are much more well informed about a topic than they are, because of internet searches at home, books and television programmes. On occasions like these staff have become adept researchers and have found themselves to be learning alongside the children or the child/children becoming the educator/s or both. Staff teams have become comfortable with this way of working and it has released them from having to be 'all knowing'; at the same time it has increased the self-esteem of the children who develop a confidence in their own ability to learn and to know how to learn.

However, in our enthusiasm to move away from an adult-led approach, the possibility that the adult could provide a provocation for learning that led to a sustained interest by some or maybe all of the children was initially misunderstood and overlooked. In this, as in all other aspects of their practice, staff teams encourage the children to use the language of learning in conversation with them and with each other and associated language such as research and researchers. We celebrate how developing children's own interests has liberated children and also staff teams to be collaborators in the learning of each other.

Getting to grips with learning groups

In our first book we were struggling to find our way with taking this approach forward. However, as we became more confident with the children's interests leading our practice and began to tune in to the fact that, at times, several children wanted to pursue the same interest, it provided the impetus for us to research and implement this method of supporting children to learn together. We had also observed on subsequent visits to Reggio Emilia how empowered children became when they shared knowledge and understandings about a given topic within a group. Different early years settings implemented this at different times, some being brave enough to give it a go at once, others wanting to gain information and confidence from those who put their toe in the water first. Implementing this way of working raised many issues since it sometimes meant that other well-established routines had to be reorganised or integrated to accommodate the learning-group philosophy into usual practice. One example of this was staff raising the question: How could you operate a key group system when you also had a learning group to support? This seemed a valid query, but in fact as experience with learning groups grew it became clear that they could be mutually exclusive when in fact they seldom were, since key groups intermingled with learning groups and flexible patterns of working by the staff teams meant it was not the difficulty that it appeared to be at the outset. Many other questions have been posed about implementing a learning-group philosophy, such as: What happens to the other children who are not involved with this learning group? Quite simply they are not interested in this topic but can contribute if they want to, but if not, they will be developing an interest elsewhere, either on their own, or with other children, which will be supported by staff members. Parents also want to know the answer to this question and to how working within a learning-group philosophy is supportive to their child's learning. With this in mind, discussions about this have become part of induction processes in nurseries across the Council area. An important motivation for staff when different working patterns or other issues arose that had to be negotiated was how much the children's learning became visible when they were working within the same group over a period of time. Many projects have been developed over the years with particular learning groups taking forward specific interests that have been made visible in a variety of ways and across different media forms. They have been exciting and have revealed children's learning in a way that has been, at times, breathtaking in its depths and understandings. Within the group children have shared ideas, theories and learned how to listen and respond to their peers in a way that they had not learned to do previously. They have also learned how to be critically analytical of each other's way of representing aspects of learning, in a way that is constructive and helpful to the group project. Most staff teams have become much more confident in embedding a learning-group philosophy into their thinking and practice with magnificent outcomes for children. We celebrate this on children's behalf and on our own!

Making children's learning visible: gaining more understanding of its purpose and practice

Through our growing confidence in developing children's interests as a platform for learning within, at times, a learning-group context we have understood how important it is to make this learning more public. What we mean here is that there is a difference between making documentation public and the ongoing documentation throughout the episode or the project. In ongoing documentation a mix of strategies are used that include recordings of dialogue, narrative and children's representations, for example. When going public, a sifting of information usually takes place and decisions are made about what will be published. In this decision-making process it will be the transparency of the learning which shows coherence and progression that will be key to its publication.

Previously we could be said to have kept this within the confines of the setting and the family, but have now understood that by making it visible across many media forms it makes it accessible not only to children, families and staff teams but to a wider audience beyond the setting. To do this, staff have learned to engage with various ways of making the learning visible and we have always been clear that there is no set way of doing this. It will vary according to the nature of the project or episode and the context of the setting. Children's representations, children's and staff narratives, PowerPoint presentations, wall panels, photographs, folders, and various technology visibilities like video clips, animations, television screens, digital frames and hand-held devices for example, have all made a rich contribution to the way in which it has been possible to make visible children's learning. These varied visibilities have been displayed clearly within the settings but also on many occasions in the communities where the children reside. Through these means it is hoped that the wider public can become familiar with the capabilities of young children and see them as being people who have a distinct contribution to make to the community where they live. Making the children's learning visible across the various media forms has required staff teams to reflect how best to do this within the context of their own setting and in a way that takes account of the audiences it is meant to serve. It has also meant that staff have needed to update themselves on the technologies that support making learning visible, since this has not been an area with which they were particularly comfortable in the past. As we know, children very often have a confidence with this that adults lack. They have learned to raise their game with this alongside the children, each learning from the other. Making children's learning visible has also caused staff to move away from descriptive captions like 'We went to the shops today' underneath an image or representation, to thinking about what was learned during such a trip and adding this to their narrative about the experience (more about this later). Importantly, reflecting more on the learning than previously has meant there are many more conversations being engaged in among staff teams, children and families about it than previously. We feel that making children's learning visible has opened up a new dialogue among educators about learning within and across settings, which has required staff to be more thoughtful about what learning is, what it can look like and how best to record it.

This aspect of implementing pedagogical documentation has required educators to have the courage to make public the work of the children and their interpretation of it to a wider audience and therefore greater scrutiny. A very public example of this was when in 2010 we collaborated with most early years settings to present an exhibition in the local Arts Centre to celebrate 10 years of working with pedagogical documentation. The exhibition was called 'Making the Joy of Learning Visible' (more about this later).

Projects and episodes: a developing confidence

Projects and sometimes episodes have become some of the main vehicles for making children's learning visible. It is important to say here that for distinction purposes we have decided to call topics that go on for a length of time, say 3 to 12 months and longer, a 'project' and those that are short lived we refer to as 'episodes'. What we have found is that episodes have a greater currency when documenting the learning of children under the age of three. Engaging with these ways of developing children's interests has required a major shift for educators since, in a previous professionalism, there was an orthodoxy that embraced the monthly adult-led theme ethos within most of the settings, regardless of whether it had run its course or not. To now move to developing a project/episode based on an identifiable and sustainable interest from a child or children that was not restricted to a time limit within a learning-group culture was both challenging and exciting. When this aspect of pedagogical documentation was gradually engaged with, again at different times across the years by different settings, there was much discussion about how this could be developed and what could support its continuation for a protracted period of time, if it required this. Clearly this had implications for how the systems of the settings worked and again there was uncertainty about how one topic could be supported if the children's interest was to be maintained over a long period of time.

At various points, professional dialogue sessions have focused on the issues that working with projects has raised. Educators have shared how they have encountered projects and how, when they have lasted over a long period of time, children, parents (at times) and educators have provided the provocations that have allowed the project to continue meaningfully, because the children's research still had a vibrancy and sense of enquiry that had not yet been satisfied.

Many of these projects have been recorded in a variety of visibilities, some on PowerPoint presentations, some in large and small folders, and others on television screens and now hand-held devices, for example. These visibilities have been shared across settings, with families and those from outside the Council area, and have been really powerful in helping all the audiences involved to gain a greater understanding of how they can bear witness to children as capable learners as well as protagonists in their own learning. They also help to showcase different ways of revealing children's learning that is both meaningful and understandable, but never patronising. (In another chapter of this book, we have updated a long-term project 'The Mural', which has continued to be developed over a 10-year period and still continues to this day.) Another important benefit of long-term projects is that they lend themselves when, in the children's final year at nursery, they become an important transition tool that accompanies the children into the first stage of primary school where they are developed further. We celebrate our growing ability to continue to learn how to develop and use projects in diverse ways to highlight children's capabilities in a way that helps others to be more thoughtful about how they engage with children wherever they encounter them.

A hybrid pedagogista post was launched

In Stirling Council it had been the practice over a number of years to appoint a teacher to most nurseries within the Council area to work alongside other staff members who had a different qualification. In 2007, it was decided to develop another role for these teachers, which was in part modelled around the pedagogista role in Reggio Emilia. Within our culture and context it was a hybrid of theirs in that the pedagogistas were allocated to three early years settings, with one of their main remits being to support the ongoing development of pedagogical documentation within each of their settings. Unlike their counterparts in Reggio Emilia, their role was localised and did not encompass a central role. This was an important and exciting innovation that supported the embedding of pedagogical documentation at the local level, which was a great support to all staff teams once it was understood exactly what their role was! (More about this in our new book, *Reggio Emilia Encounters: Children and Adults in Collaboration*, published in 2015.) That this was able to happen was a cause for great celebration, and though their role has been reorganised several times since, they still remain highly influential in the development of pedagogical documentation across the Council area.

An artist is introduced

2007 was a year of innovation in terms of additional support that was introduced to support the ongoing process of implementing pedagogical documentation. Brian Hartley, an artist, was appointed in a part-time capacity to support staff teams in developing their approach to making children's learning visible. His role was to help staff teams and children with whom he worked on site to support their growing understanding of how to use cameras and other technologies like Digital Blue effectively. With educators he was able to show them first and foremost how to use the camera to the best advantage and also how to use techniques on it to provide much more expressive images of the children's learning experiences when they were being made visible across a range of media. He interacted with the children by showing them how to use the camera in authentic ways as well as ways which were particularly exciting and attractive to them, e.g. using enhancing techniques to give an image of either a person or an object a different dimension. This allowed the children to contribute to their own visibilities within folders and journals that could be viewed by staff and families and other people visiting the nursery.

This was another innovation that we celebrated since it enriched the ability of staff to make children's learning visible in a much more meaningful way as their confidence with the camera and other technologies increased.

What has been highlighted here with joy are those aspects of our developing practice that we have been able to reflect on and at times celebrate, because we feel we have reached a new understanding. Celebration is important in this journey and not to be overlooked because other aspects of pedagogical documentation still continue to challenge us and can make us uncertain about where we go next.

What have been our ongoing and current challenges?

Re-focusing our pedagogical base

To do this, one of the first premises that we had to confront was our previous focus of working to a child-centred approach to children's learning. While this sounds similar to how we work with pedagogical documentation, it was widely misunderstood and applied. One of the terms akin to this that we began to use that was more helpful to educators was 'putting the child at the centre of her/his learning'. This was then helpful to us in implementing pedagogical documentation, since it connected well with the child's interest leading the learning. This linked with other pedagogical changes, such as developing a different value base, which, though similar to that previously held, required a considerable amount of professional dialogue and support to implement change and eventual acceptance from staff teams. As mentioned earlier, we did eventually come to see that adopting a connected set of values to those previously held was fundamental to the paradigm shift that had to take place in order to implement pedagogical documentation across all early years settings. This has been a gradual process and has meant that revisiting our value base and what it means for our work with children and families has been an ongoing process. To facilitate this, most staff teams ensure that it goes on the in-service day agenda at least once a year so that their application can be evaluated and their implementation and possible impact can be more fully understood. As part of this shift in our pedagogical base we have always known that, while we are a Reggio-inspired community, we will adopt pedagogical documentation within our own cultural context. This is important and means that how we engage with it takes account of this and so we have made our own decisions about how we apply it in practice. Always at the forefront of our minds is that living the values is crucial and the other visibilities of it will be fine-tuned according to a Scottish context whose culture will define certain characteristics of the approach. Politically, we have also had to be aware of the education climate in which we live and work and the expectations that national regulation requirements place on us. In Scotland, Curriculum for Excellence is the guidance document that all sectors of education are expected to take account of in their everyday practice. However, we are fortunate in that the values and principles it aspires to are broadly similar to those for pedagogical documentation. This is no coincidence since Linda Kinney, co-author of this book, was deeply involved in developing these at its foundation stages. Nevertheless, taking account of this curriculum guidance remains a challenge since the detail of the guidance can be misunderstood and feels as though it runs counter to what we know and understand about children's learning. This causes staff to be anxious about pedagogical documentation, since they feel that when they are inspected by HMIE/Care Inspectorate, Education Scotland their practice will not be understood nor seen as best practice. Recent inspections have proved this theory to be wrong since inspectors have been very positive about pedagogical documentation, seeing it as facilitating Curriculum for Excellence rather than the opposite of this.

Staff teams, until they have this experience themselves, will continue to see both these approaches as challenging in their implementation, rather than believing in their fundamental values and principles being an expression of each other.

We looked at some particular aspects of the pre-school centre's recent work, including the quality of the documentation approach and how it facilitates and supports Curriculum for Excellence, how educators know children are making strong progress and share the quality of work with parents.

(HMIE/Care Commission Report, 2014)

Part of our response to educators feeling under pressure about this has been to discuss with them the importance of being able to articulate confidently the vision of pedagogical documentation for children, families and the wider community; also the ability to reveal, through making children's learning visible, how capable children are in their everyday lives in the early years setting.

Negotiating the layers of making children's learning visible

Making children's learning visible has been a constant challenge to the educators across all early years settings. It had been common practice for staff to write a description or caption of the experience being shown. This was not necessarily making the learning visible and many professional dialogue sessions have focused on this aspect of documenting children's learning. It is never easy to move away from long-embedded, accepted practices and negotiate a different way of constructing who children are and how to make that visible. So we have found it to be. To some extent this has been one of the most difficult challenges and continues to be so. At its core there are many layers that have to be negotiated in making children's learning visible. First, depending on the visibility, we have to be clear why we are deciding to record a particular event or situation across any media form, whether it be a narrative, image, video clip etc. Second, this requires us to remember that it is the learning we are meant to be capturing, and if we can merge both the experience and the learning then this becomes more meaningful for the audience who are viewing it. Third, how to recognise, record, analyse and evaluate significant learning has been a cause of much dialogue on site, in courses and in one-to-one situations. It continues to be so.

Importantly, we have to be able to match the text about the experience and the individual child's or group's learning to the images, narrative, representations, for example, that we are documenting, remembering to take account of the audiences for whom we are making this visible.

Publication, as it applies to making children's learning visible, carries with it an important responsibility because it means going public with all that this implies for children, families and staff. In revealing the learning of children, it also has the capacity to showcase what educators understand about learning and its processes, in relation to the children and to themselves. For this reason, what staff have understood about their own learning in relation to what the children have learned is also important to record, albeit under a separate section of the documentation. To reach this level of documenting requires the adults to use their knowledge of each child that has built up over a period of time through interactions, collaborations and observations, for example; then, to skilfully analyse and evaluate what they see, hear and document, thereby enabling them to identify and make transparent the actual learning of each child as an individual or as a member of a group. In all of these recordings, of great importance is the capacity of staff teams to ensure that their visibilities, in whatever form, are accessible to the audiences they are meant to serve so that they give a transparency to the work of the children and the early years settings that they represent. Managing the forms of documentation for different audiences is a challenge, since we have to be mindful not to record them in strictly professional language forms but in a way that makes sense to the children, families and the community whom the setting serves. One of the current struggles around this is to find a way that does not mean recording a different narrative for different audiences, but to develop a text that will suit a variety of different audiences, thereby making it more manageable timewise. These layers of making learning visible taken together mount a significant challenge to staff teams and continue to be a source of prolonged negotiation. However, there is a positive side in that staff teams come together, whenever possible, to develop shared understandings of how the process of making children's learning visible can be transparent and accessible within a context that is manageable. This aspect of pedagogical documentation has a toxicity to it, because while it is exciting at one level, at another it is scary because it has the ability to make us feel, at times, uncertain. As human beings we like to get things right: feeling we could be wrong in our interpretation of situations and events with children's understandings makes us feel vulnerable and exposed often in a very public space.

Making assumptions

What we have come to know, often to our dismay, is that we observe children closely in the setting and notice over a period of time that a particular interest is emerging with either one child or several. We have found ourselves jumping to conclusions about what the real interest is: Is it what is obvious or does it have another interpretation? This is a question we are now posing to ourselves having made assumptions in the past that, on reflection, have found us pursuing a line of enquiry that was not really at the centre of the child's interest. On account of this, we are listening more deeply and entering into conversations with the children about their interest so that we can discern the true nature of it and resource it appropriately. This of course is more possible when children have verbal language, but when it is non-verbal we have to be particularly vigilant in what we observe and understand from the child's other modes of communication. In attempting to overcome such misunderstandings we have also become much more aware of the part that children's dispositions can play in communicating to other people what they truly want to research and pursue in relation to a particular interest that they may have (see the chapter on Shihan in this book). In relation to this, staff need to be encouraged to take their time when making these decisions, making observations, and consulting with the children, other colleagues and their families. Analysis always has to be the byword in our deliberations.

Time

While we subscribe to Rinaldi's view that time can be constructed as a value, finding it to embrace a changing pedagogical base with time-consuming elements like documenting children's learning in quite a different way to previously has presented all staff teams with a big challenge. It is something that frequently emerges in professional dialogue encounters, and various solutions have been proposed and trialled, but the different contexts in which the early years settings exist are so diverse that it is not possible to suggest a 'one size fits all' solution. The variety of ways in which time for actual documentation have been found and the discourse that needs to take place alongside it have been very creative. These are regularly shared across settings when opportunities arise in both formal and informal dialogue sessions. Of prime importance, we have understood, is the flexibility of educators in accommodating impromptu situations where capturing significant moments for a child requires time out of usual routine situations for a particular member of staff to document what has been captured. To do this, staff teams have had to reconsider how they use their time and for many it has meant moving away from inflexible routines that were restrictive in terms of accommodating a new paradigm. This has been a painful and challenging journey for many of them, but it has been one to which they have gradually responded when they have been able to see how giving time to documenting children's learning has revealed how capable and competent they are. We recognise 'finding time' as an ongoing challenge, to which we will always need to be responsive and creative, but it is one that also continues to make us thoughtful and reflective about how to find it!

Although our encounters with these challenges are provocative and sometimes make us feel uncertain, we continue to grapple with them and be thoughtful about how we can confront them. This process, while it can be daunting at times, is made to feel more manageable when we come together as colleagues and realise that we can all be having a tussle with similar issues. This does not reduce the nature of the challenges but there is always a reassurance in this.

Sustaining pedagogical documentation

Since the inception of this approach in 2000 we have developed a number of ways to develop and sustain it with educators and managers across early years settings. None of it is rocket science, but what we would suggest is that they have been ongoing up to the present day. We think this is key to its long-term sustainability since as we unpeel each layer we uncover another and staff teams need to have the security of knowing that there will be support and professional development opportunities to sustain them in this continuing and seemingly never-ending process.

Professional development opportunities

These have taken many forms. First, a variety of courses have been developed and shared with educators across Stirling over the past seven years. To support some of these courses, and to help to develop a deeper understanding of the Reggio-inspired approach, a module has been developed, funded by the Bernard Van Leer Foundation, three units of which give a deeper meaning to what working with this approach means. This is a post-graduate module which has provided a very challenging but thoughtful forum for educators to learn through professional dialogue sessions, group activities and application to practice expectations. Many staff have had access to this opportunity and have found the actual module folders themselves to be of lasting usefulness to them long after the course has been completed.

Other course themes have matched key priorities that have emerged over time, such as Learning: What is it? How to make children's early learning visible? Creativity, Critical Enquiry, Documentation as an Expression of Curriculum for Excellence, Living our Values, Pedagogical Documentation: Democracy in Action and so on. These themes were in the main determined through consultation with staff teams and also on the basis of what we understood were concerning issues for staff when we found ourselves in conversation with them on a variety of occasions.

The foundation of a Reggio-inspired network several years ago has provided another forum for us to develop our practice. It has meant that a number of staff come together three times a year to share ideas and concerns about certain aspects of their practice. Together we try and decide which topic will be our focus for these encounters; sometimes these decisions can be overtaken by other questions that might emerge in the intervening time. We relate our discourse, where it can connect to the International Reggio Emilia Network of which we are a member. This is really important, since to feel that we have a relationship with other countries working with this approach adds another dynamic to our work that feels both special and reassuring at the same time.

Allowing us to develop this international relationship further, Bernard Van Leer funded Stirling to develop a joint project with Pedagogiekontwikkeling, an early years organisation in Amsterdam. This project was entitled 'Listening to Children under Three'. This involved a nursery in Stirling linking up with one of the nurseries in Amsterdam to pursue this line of enquiry. This lasted for 18 months and involved both sets of staff exchanging visits to the respective nurseries in each country. During these visits there was a rich exchange of dialogue between both staff teams, which was both exciting and illuminating. Stirling gained insights into how the Amsterdam nursery interpreted pedagogical documentation within the context of a Dutch culture and from their own understandings of the approach. This was sometimes different to ours, which spawned healthy exchanges between educators and emphasised that there is no blueprint for the everyday practice. The only certainty is living the values that largely both nurseries had in common. The culmination of this exchange was a DVD, which represented the practice of each of the settings in relation to listening to very young children. This has been used to stimulate dialogue about how we listen to very young children, and how important it is for us to tune in across a number of communication forms in order to understand them and to support and access them to meaningful learning opportunities. It has also served as an example of our internationality and as a reminder that giving visibility to children's learning is not universally recorded in one form. It can take many forms as long as the message about how capable children are from the earliest age is clear.

Another important model of professional development is of course the on-site discussions that take place day in and day out across all settings. To give these another dimension, external consultants have also led such dialogues, which can be more focused than some of the more informal discourse that take place on a daily basis between staff teams. These have been of short duration and how useful they have been is yet to be discussed and a decision taken as to whether they will continue to be pursued as a viable form of professional development. However, with current budget constraints this model may have an appeal that is not necessarily how its usefulness should be assessed.

The exhibition organised in 2010, a great celebration though it was, provided us with another rich vein of thought to reflect on and consider what ultimately provided us with another professional development opportunity. One of the important criteria for contributions to it was that they were to represent where each setting was in their practice and it was not about showcasing the best, whatever that was considered to be. We found this to be helpful in giving staff the courage to provide their documentation and it also gave us a platform for what was to follow. While one of the main reasons for mounting the exhibition was to celebrate 10 years of working with the Reggio-inspired approach, there was another element to it that we did not immediately envisage as being part of it. Our colleague Liz Greig suggested that it would be helpful if the contributions to it were analysed so that current gaps in our thinking and understanding could be identified. These were that the coherence and progression of learning was not always apparent, the text did not always match the images and representations, and the description of the experience could still take precedence over the learning. Liz conducted the analysis, which was very helpful and provided another dynamic to fuel our professional discourse within a number of courses focused on the gaps that the exhibition revealed. It is important to say here that some staff found this analysis painful even though common key gaps emerged throughout all of the contributions. We found this to be interesting, but we also felt that the commonality of them would be helpful to staff in accepting what emerged from the analysis. It is also important to say here that the courses helped all staff, including those who were particularly affected by the analysis, to recognise how helpful it was to everybody to realise that there were common issues with which we were all struggling and that to have the opportunity to work together in a solution-focused way was very helpful overall.

Sustaining pedagogical documentation through professional development contexts: to summarise

One of the important understandings that we have developed in the area of professional development is that to be effective it needs to be constructed across broad lines of engagement. What we mean is that for teams to embrace and believe in a new approach such as pedagogical documentation, courses, seminars, however powerful, can only have a limited impact on actual practice if they are not supported by consistent in-house support. This can come about through the leadership and strong belief of the management team in ensuring that meetings of staff teams provide real opportunities for the staff to engage in professional dialogue sessions. A professional reading library within the setting is also a vital resource in supporting staff teams to elaborate their understandings of the approach and to share these with other members of staff, often for consolidation purposes. In addition the availability, on a regular basis, of an external person with an expertise in pedagogical documentation is important to endorse or give clarification to elements of the approach that are puzzling to educators. In this regard, the pedagogista role becomes a key component of a professional development strategy that overall has the capacity to, in real terms, help embed pedagogical documentation into actual practice. Neither of these standing on their own has the capability to do this, but together they can.

Where does this leave us?

It is our hope that in updating our experience of working with pedagogical documentation over the last 7 years in Stirling in Scotland we have been helpful in supporting others on a similar journey to keep faith with the vision, even though the road, at times, is considerably bumpy. We have strived in the preceding pages to be honest about where we are now, what have been our celebrations and challenges, and how we have attempted to confront them all. The reward is always how important working with pedagogical documentation is for children and families in giving visibility to the richness of children's competences and resourcefulness. How we would describe our current status is as still in a state of becoming those educators that pedagogical documentation requires us to be, and still in transition to a complete transformation of our practice. We continue to strive!

Chapter 1

Why the documentation approach to early learning?

> Documentation can be seen as narratives of children's and teachers' lives; they are a way of telling the story of one's contribution to a community.
>
> (Dahlberg 1999: 182)

Why documentation?

The documentation approach to early learning in Stirling was able to take root because it fell on fertile ground in that it connected with a way of thinking and working that already existed within Early Childhood Services. An ethos of respect and participation between adults and children was established from the outset, with organisational and curriculum approaches based on children's rights and the belief that children should be at the centre of decisions about their learning and development.

A commitment to listening to children and consulting with them is core to curriculum thinking, development and practice in early childhood settings. This was greatly influenced by understandings gained from a Scandinavian trip in 1998 and, as a consequence, a range of methods to support children's participation is in place to ensure that their voices, their views and their understandings can be heard and made more visible, so that adults can respond appropriately.

Our belief is that children have the right to be heard and have important things to say and to tell us, but, as adults, we need to be able to understand the messages that children are giving to us.

Reading about inspirational practice in Sweden and New Zealand through books like *Advanced Reflections of Reggio Emilia*, *Beyond Quality in Early Childhood Education and Care* and *Te Whariki*, the New Zealand curriculum document, made us review the approaches we were taking.

Visiting Reggio Emilia made a significant impact on us and caused us to reflect more deeply on how we could be more effective in hearing, seeing and feeling what children were communicating to us.

Our desire was to make the process of how children learn and what they were learning more visible. As part of this process, we began to 'document', to systematically record through a range of media resources including photographs, videos, journals and audio recordings what children were telling us. It was this aspect of the process and the methods of listening to children that led us to a new stage and to new and deeper understandings about:

◆   how children learn and construct meaning;
◆   the amazing ability and potential of children;
◆   ourselves as adult learners and our interactions with children and with each other;
◆   the cultural importance of families and communities.

And so began our encounter with 'documentation'. An encounter already in process through core curriculum practices like consulting with children and listening to them but in need of deepening through specific guiding principles which we understood, through our connections with Reggio Emilia, to be significant for its further development.

These guiding principles are as follows:

The rights of children should be respected

This includes the fundamental right to be heard and to have views taken into account. It means that we should not only understand the UN Convention on the Rights of the Child,[1] but be able to demonstrate, to show actively and positively in our policy and practice, how this can be achieved.

> States Parties shall assure to the child who is capable of forming his or her own views the right to express those views freely in all matters affecting the child, the views of the child being given due weight in accordance with the age and maturity of the child . . . The child shall have the right to freedom of expression; this right shall include freedom to seek, receive and impart information and ideas of all kinds, regardless of frontiers, either orally, in writing or in print, in the form of art, or through any other media of the child's choice.

Adults should be able to listen and respond

Children give us information in many different ways. It is important to ensure effective ways of supporting children to communicate their viewpoints and for us to learn the many different ways of 'hearing' children. This means actively listening to and observing children's reactions and responses. It means taking appropriate action that is visible, that can be recorded, shared, discussed and reviewed with others. It also means that we must acknowledge and confront power relations between children and adults.

> Taking action takes courage. Taking action as result of listening to children means sometimes having to change decisions already made. It sometimes shows up gaps in our adult thinking and understanding. Taking action means that we have to recognise and acknowledge this or admit that we were wrong and, perhaps more importantly, that we do not have all the knowledge.
>
> (Kinney quoted in Clark *et al.* 2005: 122)

Children as participators

Encouraging choice supports children's participation in practice as it offers, in particular, opportunities for independence and interdependence; it offers time to think, to interact, to relate and to make connections. This means recognising that a wide range of opportunities and experiences should be available to support children's participation and to assist the ways in which children learn and engage with each other and with adults.

Children as active social agents

This includes recognising that children are active participants in their own learning. It means putting children at the heart of the learning process, ensuring that they are fully involved in planning and reviewing their learning alongside the early educators, that they can engage in meaningful exchanges with adults and other children in such a way as to extend their ideas and viewpoints.

Children as meaning makers

Listening to children provides us with many valuable insights and understandings. It helps us to focus our attention on the ways in which children make sense of their world. We witness how children make connections, develop theories, construct hypotheses through the range of experiences and activities offered to them. From our careful observations and dialogue, we understand that children naturally and actively engage in the search for meaning and, in doing so, are in a constant process of constructing meaning.

Children as co-constructors of learning

The methods and approaches that support children to be central to their own learning mean that early educators can see more clearly the processes of learning, the strategies that children use and their individual personalities and interests. As educators guide and scaffold children's learning, new understandings are reached, including that the adult's hypothesis on what children are learning may not be the experienced learning of the child. The ability of the early educator to 'tune in', to interact meaningfully with children and other educators, means that, essentially, space is given to children to construct their learning alongside the adult and that children and adults can then become co-researchers and co-constructors of learning.

The pedagogy of listening

Reflecting on methods of listening to children has meant a new appreciation of what it means to listen. This has led us to contemplate and explore the multiple forms of listening, internal and external, and the complexities, both social and political, around listening. At the heart of these deliberations is Loris Malaguzzi's theory of 'the hundred languages of children' which offers to us a deeper understanding of listening as a 'culture and as an approach to life'.

The Hundred Languages of Children

The child
is made of one hundred.
The child has a
hundred languages
a hundred hands
a hundred thoughts
a hundred ways of thinking
of playing, of speaking.
A hundred ways of listening
of marvelling of loving
a hundred joys
for singing and understanding
a hundred worlds
to discover
a hundred worlds
to invent
a hundred worlds
to dream.
The child has
a hundred languages
(and a hundred hundred hundred more)
but they steal ninety-nine.
The school and the culture
separate the head from the body.
They tell the child:
to think without hands
to do without the head
to listen and not to speak
to understand without joy
to love and to marvel
only at Easter and Christmas.
They tell the child:
to discover the world already there
and of the hundred
they steal ninety-nine.
They tell the child:
that work and play
reality and fantasy
science and imagination
sky and earth
reason and dream
are things
that do not belong together.
And thus they tell the child
that the hundred is not there.
The child says:
No way. The hundred *is* there.

(Malaguzzi 2000: 1)

The image of the child as rich and resourceful

Listening to children has changed the way in which we think about children. It has changed our understandings and perspectives about how and what children learn and our image of the child. We have been able to see more clearly the amazing potential of all children, their richness, their talents, their understandings and views of the world, their feelings about themselves and other children around them as well as the adults who engage with them. 'Our image is of a child who is competent, active and critical, therefore, a child who may be seen as a challenge . . . This child is a person' (Rinaldi quoted in Gandini and Pope Edwards 2001: 51).

The guiding principles described above and the approaches that underpin them involve children as individuals, children as part of a learning group, and children and early educators as partners together in environments that inspire, that support and promote discourse, dialogue and a documentation approach that records the search and tussle for meaning.

Note

1   UN article 12, 13 (1990).

Chapter 2

What do we mean by the documentation approach?

It makes visible (though in a partial way, and thus partisan) the nature of the learning processes and strategies used by each child.

(Rinaldi 2006: 68)

What can this mean for children?

Our current cultural understanding of this pedagogical approach recognises that it makes children's learning visible and encourages them to become central to their own learning.

In real terms, this means that the child is actively involved in making decisions about which learning processes he/she engages with. On the basis of this, the educators and the child (children) through a collaborative process negotiate the context for learning together. This collaborative relationship between educators and children helps the child to feel confident in sharing their profound interests with the educators and their families in the early years setting. Having such information allows educators and children to co-construct a learning environment which will support and develop these interests across the curriculum. In this way, educators, over time, will free themselves from previously held practices where only they made decisions about what, where and how children learned.

Once this way of working has become established, the children develop an increasing understanding of their role as consultants and participants within the learning environment rather than just consumers of it. The implication of this is that embedded in practice systems and approaches are developed which create a climate wherein having this expectation of children about aspects of nursery life which affect them becomes usual rather than unusual to the extent that children become key to decision-making processes such as the organisation of the learning environment, indoors and outdoors, and such as participating in the identification of those episodes which have the capability to be converted into projects and being involved in the resourcing of them.

The implication of children playing such a central role in the life of the early years setting means that they will gain not only an understanding of the responsibility it carries but also an understanding of the need to take time to be thoughtful when they are engaging in such important processes. Allowing for and encouraging children to take time to consider, think and put forward their ideas, opinions and solutions to problems that have been posed is fundamental to this approach.

For children, educators and families, this problem-posing and problem-solving element of this pedagogical approach creates an enquiring ethos within the early years setting which nurtures that innate curiosity that children, in the main, have in their quest to make sense of their world.

Children's confidence to approach learning in this way is helpful to them when they become members of a learning group, either as a core group member or as an interested contributor. It also means that they learn to have a point of view which they express through a range of languages and which others respect and interpret within an environment where listening to each other's voices is understood not only as respectful but also as a key requisite to the collaborative learning aspect of this approach.

Allied to this is the researching element, which requires children to find out information about a given interest from a range of sources and share what they have understood with other children, educators, parents and families. In this way, they together learn to be both thoughtful and critical about the relevance of such information to the topic being researched.

> Learning is about being a researcher. The young child is a builder of theories. The young child learns by communicating and expressing their concepts and theories and by listening to others.
>
> (Rinaldi 2002)

This act of sharing and leaving themselves open to the views and opinions of others paves the way for them to become critical thinkers who are able to engage in critical dialogue with all those involved in the episode/project. This is important since dialogue between educators, between children and with families, where they are involved, is the engine room of this pedagogical approach.

These connecting threads of the documentation approach to early learning can at times become tangled and provide a variety of challenges for all those involved. However, such provocations have the ability to provoke further understandings of the approach and the learning that is in process, such that the 'provocations for learning' themselves are quickly perceived as an important dynamic of the approach which not only present themselves during the learning process but can be devised by the educators as a further strategy for extending learning.[1]

What can this mean for educators?

> We need a teacher (educator) who is sometimes the director, sometimes the set designer, sometimes the curtain and the backdrop and sometimes the prompter [. . .] who dispenses the paints and who is even the audience – the audience who watches, sometimes claps, sometimes remains silent, full of emotion.
>
> (Loris Malaguzzi, quoted in Rinaldi 2006: 73)

What this pedagogical approach means for educators is clearly affected by what this means for children. The sense in which previously educators considered themselves as primarily 'the directors' in terms of children's learning is now no longer an option, since the guiding principles of this approach require relationships between adults and children to be reciprocal, collaborative, companionable, researchers together and above all 'tuned in' to each other.

This means that the educator needs to be able to embrace these guiding principles and believe in this way of living and working with young children. Involved in such a process, he or she might find it necessary to deconstruct previous ways of being with young children in order to construct a more collaborative approach to educators, children and families. To support the educators in this process, access to ongoing professional development programmes is crucial. Their purpose will be to support both the theory and practice of this pedagogical approach, which will contribute to their developing understanding of the implications of embedding it into usual practice.

What will become clearer to them as part of such a training programme will be how to recognise with greater clarity and understanding the significant learning processes of the children during the course of an episode or project. With such knowledge, they will be able to give these visibility through various media resources and through dialogue with the child and, very often, the families. In order to make these learning processes visible, educators need to be keen observers who are alert to learning possibilities and have cameras, camcorders and audio recorders always 'at the ready' to capture these extraordinary moments.

Making the attitudinal shift required to adopt the documentation approach to early learning can create a level of uncertainty which can initially feel disempowering for educators. In order for them to accept this, almost as another principle, ongoing support in situ is essential. Naturally, living with uncertainty will cause them to pose questions to themselves and fellow colleagues and they can at times feel that this can have an impact on them in how they relate to children, parents and families in the setting. The value of these critical encounters is their ability to generate professional dialogue whose contribution to the professional life of the setting cannot be underestimated. Such dialogue can be a source of great creativity as well as of considerable discomfort for those struggling to come to terms with both the uncertainty and the highs and the lows that the visibility of this approach confers on them. Extending these professional dialogue sessions to colleagues, parents and families beyond the setting provides a further important opportunity to share understandings and misunderstandings in a desire to deepen current knowledge about how this approach works.

To consider possible solutions and to reflect on their practice, educators need time for this reflection within the routine of a usual day. This could require creative and innovative solutions to be found to create this time both for themselves and for the children at significant points for each of them in their learning. At times, to do this requires staff teams to be able to cross conventional boundaries and to perceive problems as potential opportunities rather than obstacles that are a block to further exploration and learning.

It is also our belief that the impact of this approach on children, educators and families is such that educators almost have a responsibility, as we do, to become powerful advocates for it whenever the opportunity presents itself. To be able to do this, they need to genuinely believe in its possibilities to change lives – their own and children's – and to develop the skills necessary to present their understandings to other people.

The following represents how educators, almost instinctively, learned to become advocates for the documentation approach to early learning. A group of staff who were attending an international conference locally found themselves with groups of educators from across Scotland and beyond who were debating, in their groups and in the main body of the audience, ways of working with young children. Many of the topics under discussion ran counter to what they now understood to be good practice with young children. To their complete surprise, they found themselves advocating, in a very powerful way, the documentation approach to early learning, even though they were challenged by the uncertainties and struggles that they were encountering on a daily basis. The unexpectedness of this gave them an insight into how important the development of this approach was to themselves and, most importantly, to making a difference to young children, parents and their families.

The following represents some of the struggles that staff have had to encounter in deconstructing their previous practice and constructing new and more challenging ways of working and being with the children, each other and families.

At various stages throughout a six-day professional development programme, the staff confessed to a serious crisis of confidence in relation to their ability to make this fundamental change in their practice. The presenter was, at times, finding it difficult to engage them in interactive exchanges, and, overall, there was a feeling of uncertainty all round about the ability of these programmes to inspire and enthuse staff who were clearly struggling with some of the fundamental concepts of the approach. They would often comment at the start of a new session, 'Well, at least we have come back for more, though we are not quite sure why!' To counterbalance this, upon their return six months later to make presentations to the learning-group colleagues about their adoption of this pedagogical approach, such comments were made as:

> This has been a scary six months, but what we have found out already about children that we did not know before is stopping us in our tracks. This is changing my way of thinking and interacting with the children and the families, which in this short space of time is really making a difference to how I support children's learning. What is more, we have always found difficulty in involving parents in our area, and now we are noticing that is in a process of positive change.

What can this mean for parents and families?

What this means for families is affected by the significance of the impact upon their children. It is also affected by how information about the documentation approach to early learning is communicated to them.

What we have discovered through a period of trial and error is that it has to be a method of communication appropriate to the community where the nursery is located and that it needs to be of an ongoing nature both in terms of theory and practice. It has been our experience that in a couple of communities some parents have, in the first instance, expressed serious reservations about the implications of the approach on their children within the setting and within the family. For example, one family was expressing concern about the children being allowed to share decisions with staff about how the nursery was set out. One mother said to a member of staff, 'This is the staff's job not the children's.' Clearly seeing what an element of the approach looked like in practice surprised this particular parent. She did not welcome the idea of her child having a choice in such an important element of the nursery and saw these kinds of decisions as being exclusive to adults only. There could have been many reasons for the family's disquiet relating to their own child-rearing practices or a lack of understanding about what the staff in the nursery were trying to achieve with their child. The staff team, however, grasped this as an opportunity to explain further what this way of working with children really means now and can mean in the future for life in the setting and for the home. The use of children's journals has also been a keen source of some discussion with the parents, most of them welcoming them as an important record of their children's lives in the nursery and others sometimes seeing them as potentially an intrusive element of this approach, which they only became comfortable with over time.[2] Then again, there have been one or two other parents who were quite specific about situations in which they would allow their children to be photographed and limited the use of such photographs very often to within the confines of the early years setting.

What follows is an example of one head who had, after several attempts, eventually managed to find a way of communicating with her parents and families that was meaningful to them.

At Doune Nursery, the Head had been, for some time, seeking ways of involving the families with the documentation approach through a variety of means which drew only a limited response from them. However, after having prepared a presentation about the documentation approach to early learning for a conference, which was well received by the audience, she decided that, with some modifications, it might be a good idea to share this with families at the beginning of the new session in August. She has been really delighted at the interest and involvement from families since then, and she now says, 'I cannot believe I did not think to do this sooner.' It certainly remains her intention now to start every session with a presentation of this kind supported by ongoing inputs throughout the year.

However, other early years settings found that introducing the approach through the children's involvement in a learning group, documentation folders, children's journals and active membership of a learning group succeeded for them. In these communities, presentations of projects very often came later.

Once appropriate inductions to the approach have been found, parents and families have been invited to become active participants with their children and the educators in this collaborative approach to early learning. We have found that this is much more likely to happen when it is visibly demonstrated to them that they can be integral to this pedagogical approach.

Through dialogue with the educators in the setting, it is quickly realised that most of the interests that their child/children are pursuing stem from the home. Whilst we have always had a level of understanding of this, it has been deepened by the powerful listening and collaborative elements of this approach. One clear example of this was when James, in a busy early years setting, consistently, over a period of weeks, became absorbed in constructing houses with the large wooden blocks. Educators discussed this interest of his with his family who told them that his grandmother was having an extension built and since James was often cared for by her, he had been observing this with interest on a regular basis. What the staff team did was to ask the grandmother to photograph the extension with James and link the visibility of James's family interest with the photograph of James's construction in the setting. More and more, we have sought to make visible the link between learning at home and in the setting which has been enriching for the children and at times enlightening for the parents who can have the view that 'worthwhile learning' only takes place in an educational setting.

Equally, because of the visibility of this approach, parents and families are more naturally contributing to an interest that is being developed because, without being invited or pressurised, they are able to see where they can and would want to make a contribution to an episode and to the life of a project. Some of the ways in which this has happened have been by parents researching a topic on the Internet or, for example, by developing the interest by taking their child/children on a visit to a waterfall, which is a different experience to the waterfall they went to with the staff team. Or, it has been that they have come into the setting and gardened alongside the children and at the same time brought plants and shrubs in from their own garden. In this way, shared traces are being made visible between nursery and home. Such shared moments are captured to be included in the documentation of the overall episode or project.

Making such engagements between parents, families, children and staff teams has not only been collaborative, it has also been helpful in deepening the mutual respect between all concerned as well as becoming part of that reciprocal learning element which is another significant feature of this pedagogical approach to children's early learning. In deepening our contacts with parents and families, there is an inevitability about its impact on local communities where families amongst themselves share both their reservations and celebrations about their children's involvement with the documentation approach to early learning.

What can this mean for spaces indoors and outdoors within an early years setting?

As with any pedagogical approach, working with the documentation approach to early learning clearly has a significant impact on the spaces for learning indoors and outdoors. What we have understood is that the spaces indoors and outdoors need to reflect that nature of the approach that places a high priority, amongst other things, on children's independent learning, creativity, group and individual learning, their capabilities and need for thoughtfulness. The environment is considered as the third educator:

> We value space because of its power to organise, promote pleasant relationships among people of different ages, create a handsome environment, provide changes, promote choices and activity, and provide the potential for sparking all kinds of social, affective, and cognitive learning.
>
> (Loris Malaguzzi, personal communication 1984)

In terms of ethos, what we have found to be helpful is an environment that is flexible, aesthetically pleasing and calm in its atmosphere and presentation, inclusive with a commitment to the development of a culture of enquiry amongst the children, staff team and parents and families. For this to be possible, it must be supported by responsive educators who encourage the children to pose questions, make choices and be involved in decision-making, alone or collectively.

In terms of organisation we recommend that:

◆ it is personified by its purposeful use of space rather than by the number of resources that can be housed. The children's voices should be heard in its layout specifications, and they should have easy access to personal folders and a range of resources which are visible;

- it has responsive and flexible space where children's ability to choose and use space is provided for, including empty spaces for reflection;
- it has flexible organisation possibilities which allow children not only to plan for their session but also to accommodate both individual learners and those working within a learning group;
- it is supported by routines that do not interrupt the learning processes of children and that are regularly reviewed to be sure that they are still 'fit for purpose' for any given group of children and their unique learning styles and processes;
- it is uncluttered and minimalistic in its approach to availability of resources and furniture, so that children are able to move freely and not be constrained by an over-abundance of resources. This does not mean that the setting is not well resourced; it simply means that the use of these resources can only be enhanced by their possibilities for exploration, which is jeopardised if there are too many of them available at the same time.

In terms of resources, the following have been found to be essential:

- digital cameras for educators and children;
- disposable cameras for a range of purposes;
- video camera to capture longer sequences of learning;
- Digital Blue (basic version of the above);
- hand-held tape-recorders to further record children's and adults' hypotheses about the theories they are researching;
- overhead projector/transparencies;
- computer with Internet access and printer;
- laptop – where possible with the appropriate software to accommodate the technologies that support this approach, i.e. CD-writer, PowerPoint, video facility, web-cam, etc.;
- photocopier;
- black felt pens for recording children's narratives;
- Post-It notes for educators to record observations and for children to write labels;
- notepads to record more detailed commentaries on children's pursuits or conversations;
- flip charts for children and educators to mind-map;
- display boards/small hanging pinboards for projects to be made visible (These should be at a height for both children and adults to view and should have neutral backgrounds. For maximum visibility, these should be well spaced out and should be capable of making visible the nature of the projects being developed in the setting.);
- display areas for models which are permanent and support the possible longevity of a model or table display;
- children's personal journals;
- folders to hold significant data arising from projects undertaken within the context of a learning group;
- display space for mind mapping and planning which is at a height both for children and adults to view;[3]

◆ a fiction and non-fiction collection of books which are wide-ranging in their content and are capable of resourcing, in the main, the ongoing interests and episodes and projects of the children;

◆ a collection to which new objects are continually being added for their ability to contribute to the atmosphere of awe and wonder within the setting.

Notes

1 'Provocation for learning' means a stimulus that arises naturally within a learning experience or one that is provided by the adult to extend the learning within an episode or project.

2 Children's journals are used in a number of early years settings on a regular but not necessarily daily basis to develop an ongoing record of the child's nursery life from admission to leaving to go to school. Contributions are entered by children, staff, parents and families and can include special events, favourite drawings, pictures, dialogue recorded by staff and comments by parents and families. They contain beautiful and significant memories for the children, parents and families to carry with them for the rest of their lives. They do not necessarily find their way to school; this is a decision that the child and the families make together.

3 Mind-mapping is a method used during consultation and planning sessions with the children which makes visible through a mapping system the design and plan of a particular episode, project or experience inside or outside.

Chapter 3

What does the documentation approach look like in practice?

> 'Documentation' as content is material which records what the children are saying and doing, the work of the children, and how the pedagogue relates to the children and their work.
>
> (Dahlberg *et al.* 1999: 148)

The documentation approach to early learning has afforded us the possibility to make visible the children's learning, either as individuals or as members of learning groups, by recording across a range of media both shorter- and longer-term encounters.

Those which are shorter term are referred to in this section as episodes, whilst those which are longer term are referred to as projects. In the main, what is being shared in this section is a cross-section of documentation projects as they occurred within core learning groups. This became necessary because we realised that this way of supporting young children's learning incorporates a socio-constructivist philosophy which, we understand, has many advantages for children over the mainly individualistic approach which tended to be our previous dominant practice.

What do we mean by an episode?

An episode is an interest identified sometimes by an individual child or group of children which is not necessarily sustained or sustainable over a long period of time but which it is important to make visible because of its significance in the child's/children's learning and development. As with some topics that children can express an interest in, it may be as transitory as a day, a week, or two or three weeks and then it dies. On the other hand, it may have the possibility to be developed as a project. Close observation by the staff team and important conversations with the child or children involved will be key to understanding the nature of the interest and whether it has distinct learning possibilities within the early years setting and within the community.

What do we mean by a project?

A project is not to be understood as interchangeable with 'a theme', which would be constructed around a particular topic, very often chosen by the staff team, and would usually have a predetermined time limit. Rather, a project is to be understood as an interest identified by an individual child or a group of children, which is observed as being persistent and sustained and with no preconceived time limit. (It could have started life within what educators had thought was an episodic or transitory interest.) Some projects can have an ongoing lifespan and become what we have termed a long-term project (see below, Bannockburn Mural).

The educator or educators working with this child or children would then confer between themselves or with other colleagues about its learning possibilities, both within the nursery and their local community. On the basis of such a dialogue, a decision would be made about the viability of the project, and whether it was starting its life with a problem or problems to be solved, since this can be one of the vital ingredients determining the inception of a project. If the decision is to proceed, then ways of developing it would be discussed and agreed between the child or children and the educators and families where an interest by them was known. Once a project has been agreed, then it would be referred to as a project amongst the learning-group members which would include children, educators, parents and families.

What do we mean by a learning group?

A learning group, as we understand it, is distinct from children being engaged in experiences in parallel with other children within a usual group situation and learning alone. We have taken as our conceptualisation of learning groups the following key features from the Project Zero (2001: 286). They are as follows:

◆ The members of the learning groups include adults as well as children.
◆ Documenting children's learning processes (within a learning group) helps to make learning visible and shapes the learning that takes place.
◆ Members of learning groups are engaged in the emotional and aesthetic as well as the intellectual dimensions of learning.
◆ The focus of learning in learning groups extends beyond the learning of individuals to create a collective body of knowledge.

When using the term 'learning group' within this section, we are usually referring to a core group of children who are developing their interest together through developing hypotheses and trying out their theories according to a co-researching model with the educators and, increasingly, families. This does not mean, however, that other children are excluded from a particular project or episode. The visibility of the learning group and the actual episode or project is such that other children are able to declare an interest and contribute to the learning of the group when aspects of it are attractive to them or when invited to help solve a problem that currently seems intractable to the core learning group.

Documentation in action

An episode: light and dark

Doune Nursery is a purpose-built nursery provision in a semi-rural district of Stirling. The children who attend the nursery are in the three-to-five age range and have access to it on a mixed pattern of attendance, which includes extended day and part-time provision.

How did it start?

An interest in light and dark had been prompted by one of the children bringing in a snake torch and a luminous spider. This spider sparked an interest in other children who then brought in other luminous spiders as well as other light sources which they had discovered at home – luminous shoes, light-changing torches, T-shirts, etc.

Through close observation and by engaging in dialogue with the interested children, the staff and children decided that the availability of a dark room would provide a further provocation for learning. This was duly set up, with the inclusion of an overhead projector (OHP), and the children were then able to explore the possibilities of various light sources as well as their own: OHP, CD-player, light mirror, fairy lights, lava lamp, torches, etc.

The same core group of children sustained their interest in this type of experimentation with light and dark over a period of time, which was evidenced not only through staff observations but also by the entries made in the children's planning books on a daily basis. In consultation with the children, the educators decided that it had lots of learning possibilities, which included problems to be solved and theories to be tested out; at the very least, it was decided that this could, meantime, be considered as an episode with possibilities to develop into a project.

Arising from this light and dark interest, a learning group was formed with approximately six children and one member of the staff team as a core member.

Provocation for learning: where does the light come from?

After lengthy experimentation with the various light sources, which were supplemented from nursery and home, the children began to be thoughtful about where the light in these pieces of equipment came from.

Luminous spider

Dark-room play

Light and dark group

This process clearly led the children on to electricity. The learning-group staff member, as well as the Head of the Nursery, had a certain discomfort with this because of the health-and-safety issues surrounding electricity and its potential dangers for everybody but particularly for children. However, the interest was so strong that the educators worked with the group on this, being very clear with the children about the inherent dangers of electricity, while being careful not to detract from the learning of the group.

Bearing such safety issues in mind, it was decided in consultation with the children that it would be a good idea if a set of rules was negotiated which would ensure the children's safety when considering wall plugs and using the OHP and other related electrical equipment.

This was the dialogue that took place between the educators who were the lead staff members of this learning group. Their names are Andrea and Yvonne.

Yvonne:	We are going to talk about the OHP.
Rachel:	It makes a picture on that curtain.
Yvonne:	How does the picture get on the screen?
Rowan:	Because there is light and a mirror.
Andrea:	What does the mirror do?
Flora:	It's a reflector.
Andrea:	That's right. How do we operate the OHP?
Natasha:	Because it's on it stays on.
Andrea:	Should the children turn it off and on?
Rebecca:	No, it might break.
Blair:	It might run out of that stuff electricity.
Erin:	It might break and it might run out.
James:	Grown-ups switch it on and off.
Andrea:	What do we put on top of the OHP?
All:	Pictures.
Jenna:	And it goes on the curtain.
Andrea:	What do we do with the pictures?
Jenna:	Just look and don't go close.
Natasha:	It's hot. Just keep it on.
Erin:	Not wiggle it about.
Jenna:	'Cos you might not see the picture and it might fall off.
Blair:	It might, if you keep switching it off and on the bulb inside might break.
Andrea:	What will happen to the image?
Natasha:	It might rip.
Katie:	It might get torn.
Peter:	It might flatten the battery.
Andrea:	Now that we have talked about the OHP, can we make some rules?
Yvonne:	Look at the OHP, is it on or off?
All:	Off.
Yvonne:	What do we do first?
Natasha:	Put it on.
Andrea:	Do the children put it on?
All:	No.

Andrea:	What would we do?
Flora and Natasha:	Tell the ladies.
Andrea:	What do we tell the ladies?
Flora/Natasha:	To turn it on.
Andrea:	What do we do next?
Katie:	Not switch it on.
Peter:	Not on or off.
Blair:	After that, you have to put the picture on.
Yvonne:	What else do we have to do? Where does the picture go?
Natasha:	On the curtain.
Yvonne:	How does it go on the screen?
Flora, Freya and Natasha:	Roll it down, pull it down.
Blair:	Even if it is not down, it flashes on the door.
Yvonne:	After that, what would you do?
Blair:	Watch it.
*Seuma*s:	If you drop it, the bulb might break.
Yvonne:	Does anyone know what this is?
All:	A book.
Yvonne:	Does anyone know what's in it?
All:	Pictures.
Yvonne:	What are the pictures for?
Peter:	The projector.
Yvonne:	What do we have to do with this folder?
Jenna:	You have to put them in.
Rebecca:	Take them out.
Rebecca:	And then you see them and when it's switched off, can't see it.
Andrea:	If there is a picture on the OHP and you want to change it?
Natasha:	Put it back in here [*pointing to the book/folder*].
Peter:	It would get all scraped and all ripped.
Blair:	Take it out.
Andrea:	To put it back.

Andrea explains that the OHP gets too hot and not to touch it. The ladies may turn it off if it gets too hot. The children agree to their rules for safe play.

Provocation for learning: you can't see electricity, where does it come from?

The children then came up with various hypotheses about where the electricity came from:

Blair:	Comes from the socket over there [*pointing to the wall*].
Louise:	Comes from the road.
Blair:	It comes from under the ground, people put it there, the Council.
Educator:	Who installed the electricity?
James:	It was the electricity man.

Danger sign

Freya's warning sign

Freya's plug and wire

Louise's plug and wire

Educator:	How does the electricity get from the ground to the plug?
James:	It goes through that pipe.
Louise:	It's not a pipe it's a wire.

Provocation for learning goes home . . . and comes back!

Louise: I've been speaking to my dad about electricity. He knows all about it – electronics – he told me about electrons, how they are so small you can't see them. They go through the wires and they make electricity. It goes into everything to make it work, lots of things that need electricity [*laughs*] but not paper because that's what you draw on not plastic!

Rowan: You can only see electricity in electric balls.
Louise: Electric balls are electrons.
Rowan: With the pink electricity, if you place your hand on the electric ball, because I touched one this morning before I came to nursery, and I didn't die! I've got an idea. Let's go into the dark room and look for electrons!

Where does their research into electricity take them next?

Some of the children used the Internet as part of their research; others, like Rowan, find *The First Encyclopedia of Science*. Rowan shows the educator a picture of this book, and says, 'I found a bit on electricity. I know that's electricity travelling on the ground' (pointing to the cables). Katie and Zoe are listening to Rowan's description of electricity. Katie looks at the book and decides she wants to draw electricity.

Provocation for learning goes home again

What was becoming increasingly clear to staff during the development of this significant episode of learning was that Louise, one of the learning-group members, had a particular interest in electricity because her dad was building a new house for her family. This meant that she was actively seeing electricity being installed through the cables into her house. Since the family was engaging in conversations with Louise at home about elements of the episode being researched in the learning group, they thought it might be helpful if they invited the members of the learning group to the building site to take their investigations into electricity a stage further.

Following this visit to Louise's home by the light and dark learning group, the specific interest in electricity waned and did not develop into a project, though it could be said it inspired another project about buildings which had its genesis in Louise's new house.

Louise's electrons

Katie's picture of electricity

Rowan looking at the encyclopedia

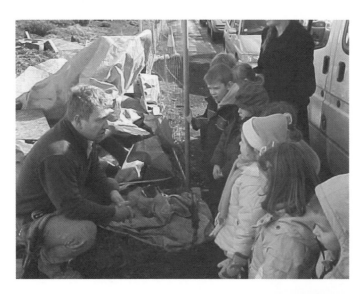

Children visiting Louise's new home

Louise's dad and electricity wires

Why this keen interest in electricity with its many possibilities for learning did not develop further will never be known. Could it have been that the children found buildings more interesting than electricity? Or could it have been that the staff team were wary of developing such an interest further, and this conveyed itself to the children? However, the significance of it was such for the learning that took place that it was really important to record it and make it visible both for the children and the parents who took part.

Documentation approach to early learning

Key features made visible

◆ Special objects brought in by the children from home provided the stimulus for this episode.

◆ The vital ingredient here was present: there was a problem to be solved, 'What is the source of the light?'

◆ Listening through dialogue and through a wide range of observations, particularly when observing children's use of torches and when children recorded dialogue, enabled the safety rules to be agreed and recorded.

◆ Staff allowed the interest to take its course and waited to see how and if it developed further, taking care at this point not to give it any direction, only to support it.

◆ Capabilities of children were reflected through, in particular, Louise's understanding of electricity to such an extent that she was able to explain and represent it verbally and through her drawings.

◆ The children were attempting to make sense and then meaning of their research into the source of light and electricity, and some children, like Louise, were able to do both, whilst others were still in the process of researching it.

◆ The children's dialogue reflected resourcefulness and creative thinking of staff and children, particularly when the staff found ways to take this episode forward when they had strong reservations about the safety aspects, like when they took the children to look at the electricity power unit outside the nursery, and the children in turn reinforced this for themselves with graphic drawings of the safety sign.

◆ Risk-taking was reflected by staff's and parents' willingness to take forward the electricity project, even when they did have concerns about safety aspects.

◆ Provocations for learning were used throughout to extend the children's thinking and learning.

◆ Home and nursery links were an intrinsic part of this episode, parents' involvement and visibility were evident throughout the episode. We now recognise visibility as an important factor in encouraging parents and families to become involved in the episodes and projects.

◆ Co-researching between children, staff and parents was evident throughout this whole process, in the use of the Internet at home and in the nursery and in Rowan's use of the encyclopedia to continue his search for more information about electricity.

An episode becomes a project: earthquake in Pakistan

The context

Croftamie Nursery is a rural nursery on the outskirts of Stirling. It currently offers provision for children in the two-to-five age group on a mixed pattern of attendance, which includes part-time and extended day provision.

How did it start?

James arrived at the nursery and joined his friend Fergus who was playing with the Lego. James was eager to ask Fergus if he had heard about the earthquake in 'Pakistani'. Fergus indicated that he did not know about this. James then began to explain that there had been an earthquake in 'Pakistani' and the school building had fallen down on top of the mummies, daddies and children.

The Head of the Nursery, Annie, was working in the office at this point and had overheard the conversation. She was interested in hearing more about this, and so she joined the children in the playroom. She explained to both children that she had overheard what had been said and was interested to hear more if they were agreeable to this. They agreed that she should join them and take part in their conversation.

James: I heard that there was an earthquake in 'Pakistani' and the ground shook like this [*James holds his hands out together and shivers and shakes, demonstrating the movement that the earthquake made*].

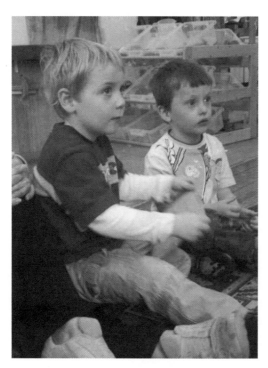

James and Fergus

Annie:	I wonder what made the ground shake like that?
James:	It's the plates moving together that makes the ground shake.
Annie:	That's interesting. Where did you hear this?
James:	I saw it on the telly and heard it on the radio in the car. The school building fell down, and the mummies and daddies and children were inside. They got squashed.
Annie:	How terrible, that must have been an awful thing to happen.
James:	Yes, and all the houses fell down, and now people do not have homes.
Annie:	How awful not to have anywhere to stay.
James:	Maybe we can help the people in 'Pakistani'.
Annie:	You would like to help them? How can we do this?
James:	I know, I have a good idea. Thunderbirds could help.
Annie:	That sounds like a good idea. How can we do this?
James:	I know. I have Thunderbirds at my house, it's 5, 4, 3, 2, 1, Thunderbirds are go!
Annie:	Good. How can they help us?
James:	Well, they're not real, Annie.
Annie:	Oh! So that won't work then?
James:	No, but I have another good idea. I could take some money from my piggy bank and send it to them.
Annie:	Well, James, I think that is a very kind thing to do, and if you take some money from your piggy bank, I'll give you some money from my purse to send also.
James:	Well, not all of my money from my new bank, just a little.
Annie:	Of course, I am not giving you all of my money from my purse, but I will give some of it. I am wondering how we are going to get this money to people in Pakistan.
James:	I know, we can send it on an aeroplane to the Pakistani people and then they can buy things.
Annie:	What a good idea. Maybe other people would like to help. What do you think?
James:	Yes, I think the mummies, daddies would like to help.
Annie:	But how can we let them know about this?
James:	Yes, I think the mummies and daddies would like to help.

Provocation for learning

Annie:	But how can we let them know about this? [*James thinks about this . . .*]
James:	I know, let's send them a letter telling them about it and ask them to help.
Annie:	What a good idea. What should we say in the letter? Would you like to tell me, and I will type it out for you and then we can photocopy this?
James:	Yes.

Fergus, who had originally been involved in the discussion for some time, returned to listen to the conversation and indicated that he would also like to help.

Provocation for learning: how can we find out more?

The Head then suggested to James and Fergus that together they go into her office and look on the Internet to see if they could get some information about the Pakistan earthquake and find ways in which they could help.

Both James and Fergus agreed that this was a good idea.

A website was found which gave the information about the Pakistan earthquake and about the resources the people in Pakistan needed. It also showed pictures of the resources that the money could buy. The three of them looked at this for some time, and both James and Fergus decided they wanted to buy resources with the money that they collected.

Having sourced this information, Annie decided it would be helpful to contact James's mum at work to share the news about her son's idea. She was eager to get her permission to take this forward. Mum agreed; however, what was not clear to us was that James's mum was so moved by her son's thoughts and actions that she took the opportunity to share it with her work colleagues. They spontaneously decided that they wanted to be involved in the fundraising.

James and Fergus then dictated the letter and then photocopied forty-four copies.

James went off to make the picture for the people who may want to help.

Forty-four envelopes were counted out and both James and Fergus put the letters into envelopes. By the end of the morning, the envelopes were ready to be given out.

James took the lead and engaged with the parents as they came to collect their children. James handed parents the letter, taking time to tell them about his ideas and how he wanted to help the people in Pakistan who had been affected by the earthquake.

James, Fergus and Annie on the Internet

James writing a letter

James drawing a picture

James and Annie put
letters in envelopes

Fergus puts a letter in an envelope

Provocation for learning: who else should we share this with?

Annie, the Head, then suggested to James and Fergus that they should share with the rest of the staff and the other children what they had been working on that morning so that they could help and be involved if they wanted to.

Annie then said to both boys, 'You have really worked hard this morning finding ways to help the people in Pakistan. Do you know that there is a name for the job that you have been doing? It is called fundraising. This means that you are both fundraisers.' James, in particular, was very happy with this and used this new word to share with his friends in the nursery. He told them, 'I am a fundraiser!'

James and Fergus sharing ideas with others

Where does the episode go next?

This interest, that started as an episode as described during one morning, developed into a project. James and Fergus, in the meantime, collected a sizeable sum of money and became very keen to include other children in their work, which meant that there was now a learning group emerging whose interests in the Pakistan earthquake were appearing to be diverse. The two staff members of the learning group were working with the children to discover what exactly sparked James's interest in the earthquake. Was it that he felt compassion for the people themselves? Or was it that he wanted to know more about earthquakes and how they happen and could this happen in his home or the nursery? Or was it both? Also they were becoming aware that other children in the learning group were definitely showing an interest in what makes buildings crumble and fall apart. What they understood already is that these different interests would continue to emerge and provide rich possibilities for learning which they would plan for in consultation with the children. And so, the project, still in its early stages, continued, and families as well as children and staff were supporting its development.

Documentation approach to early learning

Key features made visible

◆ James's keen interest in the Pakistan earthquake provided the impetus for an episode of learning to develop.

◆ The vital ingredient was present: there was a problem to be solved – 'How can we help the people in Pakistan who have no homes following the earthquake?'

◆ The listening culture within the setting meant that the Head of Nursery was used to tuning into the children in the nursery and understood that something significant was being discussed, and she followed it up.

◆ The sustainability of the episode was possible because of the enthusiasm that Fergus and James continued to have and, as a consequence, the other children became 'infected' by it.

◆ Because of its sustainability and the interest of a larger group of children, the episode proved that it had the capacity to develop into a project.

◆ Being respectful to children, the Head didn't interrupt the initial conversation and sought the children's permission before she joined them.

◆ The Head did not make assumptions about the interest but researched it further with the child and discovered James was motivated by compassion not by the technicalities of why and how buildings collapsed. It was important for the learning potential of the project for this process of 'going deeper' to take place.

◆ Listening through observations was clearly present in finding out what James's initial interest was, in order to follow it through appropriately.

◆ Provocations for learning were threaded through the project overall. These provided a real stimulus for the children and provoked them to extend their learning about the earthquake as well as helping them to solve problems when they arose.

◆ Listening as an emotional response to an encounter or situation was evident between the Head, James and Fergus.

◆ Children tried to make sense and then make meaning of this natural disaster and constructed theories around it from a variety of aspects depending on the varying perspectives of the children involved in the group. James's sense of compassion was aroused; another child was interested in how and why buildings collapsed.

◆ The co-researching element was emphasised in how staff and children used various media resources together to find out how to fundraise and how to use the money when collected. Access to the Internet was crucial in this process.

A project: the one-eyed rabbit

The context

Fintry Nursery is a nursery in a primary school which is located in a semi-rural area of Stirling. The children who attend the nursery do so on a morning-only basis and are in the three-to-five age range. There are two early years educators.

The images that follow were captured as part of a long-term project which became known as the One-Eyed Rabbit for the simple reason that the rabbit around which the project was based had only one eye.

The project started in August and continued in the nursery until the following August when the rabbit accompanied the children starting school into Primary 1 (reception class) for a six-week period.

How did it start?

Through listening and close observation, the members of staff became aware that a group of children, initially three of them, were developing a deep interest in hospital matters and, in particular, in making people better. One of the staff members remembered that her daughter had a rabbit with one eye whom she thought they might like 'to try and make better'. After discussion with her colleague and the agreement of her daughter, Rabbit came to nursery and became a provocation for learning.

Whether there are problems to be solved is a key factor in deciding whether a project has rich learning potential or not. Most of those confronted in this project are outlined below. Many of these were posed by the children, others by the educators and some in collaboration with each other.

Provocation for learning: how do we make Rabbit better?

The children soon became absorbed in how to 'make Rabbit better' and restore him to full 'rabbithood' again. Following an analysis by the staff team of the possibilities for learning within such an interest, the staff plans and children's plans began to clearly reflect this emerging project – or did they? At this point, both sets of plans merged, and, in an ongoing way, supported the organic nature of the project as it developed into expected and unexpected territories.

How did it develop?

Initially, three children came together as the core learning group who were quick to engage with Rabbit and his dilemma. This caused them initially to be thoughtful about how he came to lose an eye and then to consider the reason for having two eyes as opposed to one. This led them to consider their own images with cameras, mirrors and their own representations of themselves with two eyes. This period of intensive research and the understandings arising from it led the core group of children to enter into conversations with the rest of the children in the nursery who, as a result, included themselves in this exciting exploration.

The one-eyed rabbit

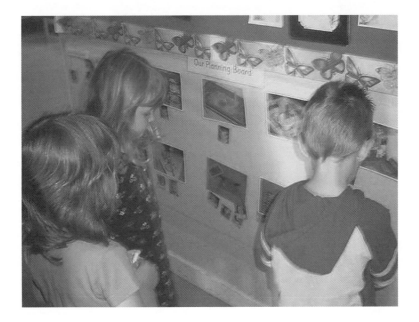

Children at the planning wall

Children reflecting on this exploration

However, this was only the beginning! What follows is an overview of the community of enquiry that developed from the introduction of the one-eyed rabbit to the nursery.

It is important to indicate that the interest in the rabbit was not confined to the core learning group. Opportunities were created for these children to regularly update and involve the other children in the setting in the avenues of enquiry as they emerged and particularly when there were problems to be solved. Those children who were not members of the core learning group tended to dip in and out of the interest to pursue those of their own. This is an important feature of working within this approach.

Provocation for learning: how to replace Rabbit's eye?

In the quest to replace Rabbit's eye, the children developed a number of theories which were shared within the core learning group as well as with the other children in the setting and their families. They put their theories into action by using materials in the nursery such as paper, pebbles, glue, string, jewels, etc., which they thought might become a substitute eye. What satisfied them as a solution at this point was black paper screwed up and stuck into the blank eye space.

Provocation for learning: replacement eye fell out – what now?

Initially, when this happened, the staff observed and listened to the core learning group and were surprised to learn that they did not seem particularly interested in pursuing a substitute eye for the rabbit. Instead, they noticed that the children were adopting really caring attitudes towards the rabbit and his condition, which the staff supported them in extending to other children in the setting.

   Until one day . . . one of the girls in the core learning group told one of the staff that her granny had suggested that a solution could be sewing a button into the space where the eye should be.

Provocation for learning: what gender is the rabbit?

Again, through systematic observation, listening and recording the children's dialogue, it emerged that two of the girls in the core learning group were keen to dress the rabbit in girls' clothes. The children's approach to this was quite simple: 'boys wear blue and girls wear pink'. This sparked a discussion about what gender the rabbit was and how this could be reflected in the clothes it wore. The educators saw this as a good opportunity to research this area of children's perceptions about possible relationships that can exist between gender and clothes in particular. This dialogue between the children and the educators was extended to include families, and it evoked a great deal of interest and sharing of clothes and photographs.

Provocation for learning: Rabbit is poorly – what can we do?

Again, through systematic observation, listening and recording of dialogue in the home corner, the staff became aware that there was a high level of imaginative play in the home corner intensely focused on the health of the rabbit. Various hypotheses were posed as to the particular health problem that the rabbit might have, and eventually the children decided that they must set up a doctor's surgery to diagnose his condition. In consultation with other children and the educators, they made their plans for constructing a doctor's surgery within the area where the home space was usually located. Rabbit then became very ill, which necessitated the transforming of the doctor's surgery into a hospital. The help of one of the mums, who was a sister in an operating theatre, was sought here, and she came in to show them how some operations are performed. More dramatic hospital role play developed from this: everybody was 'operated on', not just the rabbit, but also the children, the educators and the buddies.[1]

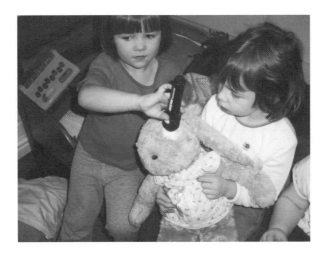

Shining light on Rabbit's eye

Fixing replacement eye

Children learning to sew

Rabbit and clothes

Mum in operating theatre

Provocation for learning: Rabbit could be dying – what does this mean?

The possibility of Rabbit dying caused the children to consider, first, how they could prevent this and, second, what does dying or death mean? The children reflected deeply, during the course of a conversation with the staff team, on what death meant to them at this point in their understanding, and there were many expressions of this through 'the hundred languages of children'. They presented their theories about death and dying to the whole group of nursery children through oral communication, and many of them were keen to illustrate their understanding through paintings and drawings, which were presented on panels and mounted on the wall near to the home corner in the nursery. Families were consulted about how comfortable they were with this avenue of enquiry, since children had different versions of what happened after death which could have proved to be offensive. There were no objections, and so a fascinating dialogue opened up which revealed understandings and misunderstandings that children might have about an area that might not often be broached with them.

Provocation for learning: how do we keep Rabbit alive?

In the search for ways of keeping Rabbit alive, the children came up with a number of suggestions. First, they thought it might be a good idea if the member of staff who brought Rabbit to nursery took him home to be nursed by his owner, her daughter. Then, after a good deal of consultation amongst themselves, they felt that since Rabbit could not be left on his own in the nursery overnight and at weekends, it would be a much better idea for each one of them to take him home each night on a rota basis. This was readily agreed by the educators, since they were keen to develop further the learning connections between home and nursery which had been getting stronger as the life of the project expanded. A special bag was created between children and staff which contained medical records, medicine and a book to record Rabbit's experiences when he went home. The response of parents to this was amazing. Children and parents pooled their resources to make this work and shared the respective outcomes enthusiastically with the members of the staff team.

Provocation for learning: Rabbit is disabled – what does this mean?

Throughout the lifetime of the project, both of the educators had been engaged in ongoing professional dialogue to support it and to consider what were the learning possibilities evident to them as professionals that were not arising as part of the consultation and participation with the children. One of these was disability awareness. The one-eyed rabbit could be considered to be disabled, and they felt it was important for this concept to be explored with the children who had not encountered this aspect of life previously within the setting. As it so happened, this was one of these coincidences mentioned earlier which they came to know about through the 'regular

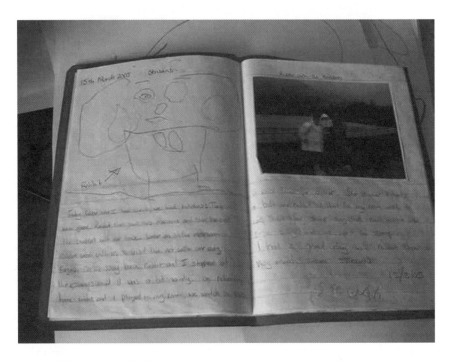

Book showing dialogue about Rabbit

children's meetings'.[2] One of the children's grandfathers used a wheelchair, and so he was invited to come into the nursery to talk to them about his disability and how the wheelchair helped him to get about. About the same time, because parents were very much connected with the project, one of them suggested that a lady in the community had disabled dogs – one of which had only three legs. She also was invited into the nursery with the dog. Finally, in this aspect of the project, an almost unbelievable coincidence occurred when one of the children shared with an educator that his granny had now only one eye; she had just had the other one removed! She also was very happy to come and share her experience of living with one eye with them.

Kieren's nana comes to visit

Kieren had been telling us about his nana who had her eye removed recently. Since we had Rabbit with his one eye, we asked if Nana would come along and talk to us about what it is like to have just one eye. She was very happy to do so!

Rosellen (Educator):	How does Kieren's nana look?
Cate:	She looks different and she has a sore face.
Kieren:	You've got hearts and bones in your body, I saw it on telly.
Rosellen [to Nana]:	What was it like in hospital?
Nana:	People were all dressed in green with masks on.
Struan:	Was your eye sore?
Nana:	It wouldn't get better, so the doctor said the only way they could make it better was for it to come out.
Jennifer (Educator):	How long did you have to stay in hospital?
Nana:	Just for one night.
Kieren:	When are you going to open your eye?
Rosellen:	Is it difficult just having one eye?
Nana:	Threading a needle is difficult, and I can't see people on my left side.
Kieren:	Nana needs a walking stick.
Niamh:	My grandpa has a walking stick.
Kieren:	So does my dad.
Cate:	Can you see the ground when you are walking?
Nana:	I have to be very careful when I am walking, so I don't fall. The walking stick helps me too.
Niamh:	Can you see all around you?
Nana:	Not very well. When Kieren plays hide and seek, I can't find him.
Pippa:	How did they get your eye out?
Struan:	Your eye is made of jelly!
Kieren:	They used pliers.
Nana:	They used special tools.
Stuart:	My eye has come out now [*pretending to close one eye*].
Kieren:	When are you going to get a new eye?
Nana:	When I go to Glasgow, I am going to see an artist, who is going to paint a picture of my good eye, and then from that they will make a new one.
Struan:	What will they make it from?

Kieren's nana with Kieren

Nana:	Well, a long time ago it would have been glass, but now it is made from plastic.
Jennifer:	Will you be able to take the eye out?
Nana:	Yes, they will show me how to clean it and put it in and take it out.
Cate:	All of us here have two eyes, and Nana has only one eye, and Rabbit has only got one eye too!
Nana:	When I get my new eye, I will come back and see you, if you would like.
All:	Yeh, thank you very much Nana for coming to see us. We can't wait to see your new eye.

Nana did return to see the children with her new eye and, since most of the children involved with this project, including Kieren, her grandson, had now gone to school, she went to visit the learning group in their new primary-school setting to share with them the next part of her experience with her 'new eye'.

The three-legged dog

Jennifer (Educator):	How did the dog lose its leg?
Stuart:	A car vroomed and ran over it.
Cate:	He went under the car.
Kirsty:	You have to be very careful when you cross the road.
Struan:	You need to look where you are going.
Elizabeth:	You need to listen with your ears, and then you know when it's safe to cross.

Jennifer:	Could the dog do all the things that a four-legged dog can do?
Niamh:	Yes, cause dogs are very clever.
Kirsty:	He went zooming fast.
Stuart:	He's got lots of energy!
Kirsty:	I threw the ball for it, and it ran really fast, just like my dog.
Rosellen (Educator):	It was moving so fast that I found it hard to take a photograph.
Jennifer:	If he only had two legs, could he still do all of those things?
Stuart:	He would fall over, and only the back ones will work.
Cate:	He would fall over . . . that's not good.
Kirsty:	What would happen if he got all his legs knocked off?
Stuart:	He could run on his tail!
Niamh:	I think he could do a handstand on his tail. [*All of the children start to laugh.*]
Struan:	He could have a walking stick.
Kirsty:	Wheels. He could have wheels! You could put them on his tummy.
Jennifer:	Have you seen a person with wheels?
Cate:	Some people have legs, but they can't walk.
Niamh:	A wheelchair.
Jennifer:	What is a wheelchair?
Cate:	It's a chair that has wheels.
Pippa:	Someone needs to push them.
Cate:	If their arms work, then they can push themselves with the wheels. [*Cate and the other children get up and try to move around the room using only one leg.*]

Three-legged dog

Cate:	It's hard only using one leg.
Katy:	My papa has got a wheelchair cause he can't walk. He's got a button on his wheelchair that makes it go. It goes back and forward.
Cate:	How does he get in the car?
Katy:	My mummy and grandma help him into the car. They hold his arm to get him into the car.
Struan:	A walking stick would help.
Jennifer:	If you only had one eye, could you see everything?
Kirsty:	It's better to have two eyes cause you look better.
Cate:	You can see better too.
Struan:	It wouldn't be very nice if you didn't have any arms or legs.
Niamh:	You couldn't play football or rugby or run very fast.
Kirsty:	You wouldn't be able to wave your arms or dance.
Struan:	You would get bored.
Pippa:	You could talk.
Struan:	If your eyes don't work, you are blind.
Pippa:	If you had no ears, you wouldn't listen.
Cate:	If you had no teeth, you wouldn't be able to eat.
Jennifer:	Let's hold that thought for another day!

The atmosphere around this project was at all times exciting, at times breathtaking in the depths it plumbed in the children, educators and families, and, wondrously, coincidences occurred that made significant connections with particular milestones in the project. Such coincidences injected a sense of relevance and realism into the overall project and made aspects of it much more understandable to the children – for example, Granny with one eye, three-legged dog, Grandfather in a wheelchair.

The children's interest in Rabbit remained alive for the remainder of the session, and what emerged, surprisingly, was that it was only towards the end of the session that they declared an interest in giving it a name. This involved the children in a consultation process which gained momentum in its remit as it went along. For example, they began to think about the rabbit's date of birth and address as well as its possible name, which eventually led them to developing a passport for it, which came in useful for the rabbit when it made the transition from the nursery to Primary 1 (reception class). The name they decided to give to the rabbit was Bouncer Hopper Shadow Rabbit.

As the nursery year came to its close in June, the one-eyed rabbit went home to his owner for the summer holidays. At the beginning of the new term, the rabbit returned to accompany the children going from the nursery to start school. This provided a continuity for the children and the encounters that the rabbit had during his time in the primary school have been recorded.

The project continues. Significant traces of the work developed through the rabbit remain visible in the nursery in various media forms, and, in time, through revisiting these, the idea is that the children and educators may well develop the project further or integrate elements of it into a future project. A further important feature of this approach is not only its adaptability and flexibility but also that time is never really called on a project – it always has further possibilities for the same children or for a new generation of children to research.

Documentation approach to early learning

Key features made visible

- An adult-led stimulus was prompted by an early interest that some children were showing in caring for others.
- The vital ingredient, a problem to be solved – 'How we can we restore Rabbit's eye?' – was clearly present at the outset of this project.
- It went beyond the episode stage because of the sustained interest of a core group of children initially, whose enthusiasm for it captured the interest of most of the children in the setting.
- Its capability to become a project was due to this as well as to the ability of the staff at times to introduce elements that they felt were particularly relevant for the children and the community. In a sense, this meant that they were adopting one of the Malaguzzi roles of the educator to 'be a director at times'.
- Such was the interest from all actors, including children from Primary 6 in the school, that it became a transition project for the children from early years nursery to early primary.
- Professional dialogue was an ongoing part of this project which took place informally and formally between two staff members. They reflected on what they had heard and what they had recorded, which enabled them to support the strands of learning as they emerged.
- The sustained use of provocations for learning was evident throughout this project.
- The staff team developed the ability to use and build on all the resources available within the early years setting, the school and the community.
- A listening culture was developed across a range of media, i.e. keen observation techniques, recorded conversations, audio recorders, video clips and profile entries.
- Learning within the nursery began to extend beyond it. It found its way into the local community and into the primary school where it engaged the support and talents of the primary head teacher.
- The early years primary staff in the school showed real enthusiasm to engage with the nursery team when the rabbit accompanied the children starting primary school in the autumn.
- A culture and ethos of enquiry developed between, particularly, the children, the staff and the families. This came about almost automatically because the children began to understand the importance of asking questions through the educators' use of them, and then they did likewise. Interestingly, parents then began to follow suit, and the educators began to recognise this as a community of enquiry and talked about it as such.

A long-term project: a Bannockburn Mural, November 1999– March 2006

The context

Park Drive Nursery is a refurbished nursery provision attached to a primary school in an urban area of Stirling where the children who access the nursery are in the three-to-five age range and attend on a part-time and extended day pattern of attendance.

This project is quite distinctive and is included because it has revealed itself as being capable of sustaining a long-term interest over a six-year period with different generations of nursery children contributing to its emergence and development. This is important because, as well as its longevity, it demonstrates that children can pause their current profound interest and, because of its visibility on wall panels, inside and particularly outside in this instance, and in folders, they and others can revisit it and bring fresh ideas and insights for its future development. One of the other advantages of such a project is that the children are engaging with their local area, which helps to keep it alive for current and new children in different contexts and with a range of people, both of which will influence the children's thinking about their community. Their expression of this will be made visible within the overall project but most noticeably within their extension of the mural itself.

How did it start?

This project arose initially from a group of children becoming interested in creating images of themselves as part of a settling-in process in the nursery at the beginning of the new term. As part of this process, they decided that they would like to be able to make bigger images of themselves, and the educator, who was leading on this interest, felt that she needed help with this herself since she knew that she did not have the skills to support them. To do this, she engaged the help of the Play Services staff team and also members of the community, one of whom she understood specialised in creating large images on different types of materials to match different environmental conditions and the other an art student who was a friend of a member of the staff team.[3]

Once the children had been exposed to the techniques shared with them by the community specialists, they developed their own large images, which are shown below. Having achieved these, they appeared to have abandoned their interest in this process.

However, it was revitalised a few weeks later when, out on a usual outing into the Bannockburn community where the nursery was located, they became fascinated by a very noticeable church building which had significant characterising features. This inspired their interest in other large buildings in their community, and the staff team, aware that there could be a connection between their interest in large images of themselves and large buildings, thought this could well be an interest that had the potential to be developed further.

Stuart's drawing of the church building is shown on page 44. This technique of sketching the church building was supported by Michelle, the art student, and the members of the staff team who had been observing the strategies used by her with the children.

The children's interest in this building then led them to become aware of other buildings in their community, and it became clear over a period of time that they had twin interests: first, their interest in large images and, second, their interest in their local area, which it seemed that they were seeing for the first time as a place of real interest.

Through conversations between the children and meetings between educators and children together, it was agreed that this had the potential to be a project exploring the buildings in the local area. Because of the children's interest in large images, it would be represented by a large mural known as the Bannockburn Mural. Although

Children painting large pictures with the artist

Children looking at and drawing car

Stuart's drawing of the church

Michelle's interpretation of Stuart's drawing

it was a core learning group of children who were involved in the project initially, the visibility of it was so powerful that all the children in the nursery contributed to the emerging mural and associated activities over a considerable period of time.

Provocation for learning: how do we fit the church into the mural?

Although the children had managed, with the help of Michelle, to draw a large outline of the church building, integrating it into a mural, which needed to represent all of those aspects of the local area that attracted their interest, was quite another matter.

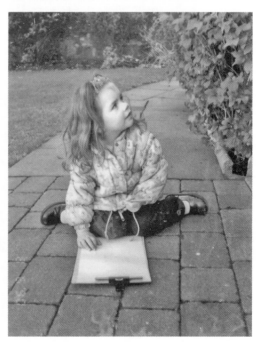

Children kneeling at church door   Child kneeling on pavement

This meant that they now had to look more closely at the features of the church, not just its impressive outline. They were exploring and looking at its features and trying in some way to represent them on paper to take back to the nursery for further discussion with the other children and educators as to how to merge the church into the mural.

Provocation for learning: where to position the mural?

Having done initial explorations into the community, important questions arose such as: Where will we hang a mural of this size? Will where it hangs affect the kind of materials to be used?

During the course of their research into local buildings, the children began to realise that whilst a large mural was a desire they had, to manage it posed some an important question: Was there a space large enough in the nursery, either inside or outside, to display it? Wherever it was, the materials used would have to be suitable for its environment, if it was to be enduring.

Answering such questions involved the children and the educators in some interesting conversations and required a facilitative and consultative approach to ensure that the voices of the children were heard as powerfully as those of the educators and community specialists.

After this process was completed, it was agreed that the most appropriate place to display the mural was outside. This was for two reasons. First, since the interest of the children was about representing the external appearance of large buildings in their community, it seemed fitting to fix it to the external walls of the nursery. Second, it was realised that if created from suitable environmental materials, it might have the possibility of becoming a permanent feature of the building. The latter really appealed to the children. It certainly had attractions for the educators also since it left traces of these children which other children would have the opportunity to pick up and relate to in their later contributions.

John cuts up lengths of black plastic

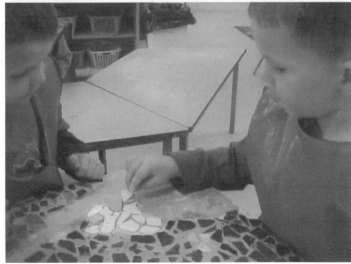

Children continue to work on mural

Interest and help from parents

The agreement on the space where this was to be hung was only the beginning of a very long process of accessing materials suitable for the outside environment and finding ways of fixing such a large mural to the external wall of the nursery building.

What follows are images of the children inside the nursery using a range of materials to develop the outside appearance of the church and its railings. Through this, the children were developing understandings of those materials which would withstand the weather as opposed to those they were familiar with using indoors.

Throughout this whole phase of the project, excursions into the local area continued at regular intervals to inform the emergence of the mural.

Provocation for learning: what kind of backdrop will support the weight of materials being used and how to plan for them on such a structure?

At each stage of this project, help from community specialists was called upon, and they became ad-hoc members of the core learning group. Consultation with them and participation by the children and the educators in the overall process was crucial to its successful development. Again, this collaboration between all key players is

Children on project excursions

fundamental to the documentation approach to early learning. From such an engagement, it emerged that large wooden boards would provide a suitable support for the materials to be used, and the space on these boards would have to be carefully planned to ensure that all the elements of interest to the children could be incorporated.

Meantime, inside the nursery, the children continued to develop elements of the mural with a variety of materials which involved them in rich and rewarding learning processes.

Again, due to the powerful visibility of this project, parents participated at various stages of its development, both inside and outside the nursery. They came into the nursery to support it both with their own children and others.

Provocation for learning: how do we fix the wooden backdrop on to the external wall of the nursery?

This became another problem to be solved. The mural had now reached a stage where all the aspects that the children had decided were important elements of the community to be incorporated had been constructed. Now came the problem of how to fix it onto the external wall. They researched and experimented with this extensively in collaboration with the educators. They tried out their theories and understood during the process what did not work and why and, eventually, what could work and why.

This collaboration of the children with each other and their co-researching with the educators is made visible in the images on these pages. It led them to an understanding, in conversation with the adults, that whilst fixing the drawings onto wood with sellotape on the outside wall did work, placing the wooden backdrop of the mural on to the wall permanently would need further expert assistance. The staff suggested that they bring in a joiner. They consulted with a local joiner who readily agreed to help them, and the mural was eventually fixed to the wall.

Lisa and Hayley blocking in the areas

Children putting work outside

Emily and Kimberley continue to experiment with sticking outside

Alex's picture with sticking tape   Local joiner fixes mural to the wall

This represented what this group of children found interesting in the local community but, as was to become evident later, the next generation of children who came to the nursery 'saw' other elements of the community that they felt should become part of the mural. This is what this pedagogical approach has to offer. Time is never called on a project; it is very visible. This always leaves open the possibility of having another dimension to it which other 'eyes can see'.

As we write, the current generation of children are about to mount their extension of the mural next to the original one. Their understandings are different to those of their predecessors but add another dimension to a long-term project which tells its own story about what interests different children about their own community and how they choose to record it.

Documentation approach to early learning

Key features made visible

- The impetus came through the children's interest in developing large drawing techniques.
- The vital ingredient was at the core of the initial interest: there is a problem to be solved, which is 'How do we draw large buildings?'.
- The mural continues to reflect the images, experiences and relationships of each generation of children. Its history is embodied in its availability and visibility.
- The mural has become embedded in the nursery culture and the community.

Current mural with additional section to the right

◆ Collaboration between children, families, professionals and the community are reflected in the project. This was particularly noticeable at the outset, when the children and the artists were working together to develop large images, the artist giving her impression of the church and the children recreating their own.

◆ The co-constructing alliance that was formed between educators, children, families and members of the community when the mural was actually being developed was very powerful. It empowered the children in their decision making about what was to be included on the mural.

◆ The decision of the staff team to invite members of the community into the project that included not only parents and families but also community specialists such as artists and joiners.

◆ Problem solving by staff and children became a significant feature of this project. This was most evident when the children were trying to find out how to attach a drawing to the outside wall.

◆ There was an ongoing use of provocations for learning throughout the life of the project.

◆ Children were listened to through observations, recorded and oral, and through drawings, oral and non-verbal communications.

◆ There was a recognition by educators that there is no need to 'call time' on a project. Its time should be measured according to the interest of the children and not by conventional term endings, etc. This should be an understood possibility when engaging with a project.

◆ Shared memories of existing children and new children helped the project to be sustained. When new children joined the nursery, the returning children talked to

Latest panel in the mural

the new children about the mural through its visibility on the outside wall and through folders which had been made about its life so far.

◆ The longevity of the project was possible because it literally became part of the fabric of the early years building. Its location on the outside wall of the nursery means that it is visible to families and the community. It is of the community.

◆ The mural is an example of an ongoing project which still has a future and has existed through six generations of children and still retains its energy. This is reflected in the completion of the next panel of the mural featured on the previous page.

Eight years on

In the intervening years since the first edition went to press there has been a continuing interest in and extension of the Bannockburn Mural within Park Drive Nursery. As previously, in considering the longevity of this project we have been reflective about what contributes to such a sustained interest over such a long period of time. These reflections have led us to reach several possible conclusions, which are:

◆ the dominant position of the Mural on the outside wall of the nursery near to the entrance;

◆ its vibrant colours and texture that has attracted children and families to look, touch and feel;

◆ its links with the community in which most of the children and families live;

◆ its ability to make children's learning visible and to cause new generations of children to raise questions about those aspects of the local community that are not represented;

◆ its continuing visibility and its ability to leave memories created by siblings of children attending the nursery at a particular period in time;

◆ possible expectations of siblings of children who had previously attended the nursery feeling that they too will make a panel for the Mural;

♦ the mind set of the staff team who continue to see this project as alive with possibilities and always having a future; and

♦ the listening culture that exists in the setting that means that educators tune into questions that children have about the Mural and explore with them what they have to offer it.

Each of these, over time, has been a contributing factor to the longevity of the Mural, but collectively they have proved to be powerful provocations and incentives for new generations of children to give expression to what they wanted to give visibility to about their community.

What have new generations of children wanted to give expression to?

The process

In the last eight years, several generations of children have contributed three new panels to the Mural. Clearly what this means is that there is always a panel in process since there is a tendency for them to be developed over a two-year period. This is not deliberate: it is dictated by the pace of progress that suits the children and which allows them to be thoughtful about their process, and consider questions that arise to which answers need to be found in collaboration with the staff team.

Since it is the ethos of the nursery to go out into the community on a very regular basis this remains an important provocation for the extension of the panel. Comments abound during these visits about the community and its landmarks, and staff are very aware of the importance of listening to these comments and questions and clearly record these as they arise for further discussion with the children and their colleagues. From such collaborations, competing community interests can emerge and time is made for the children to engage together in deciding which community element will prevail to be developed as another panel for the mural. Such encounters can have a real dynamism to them and from these exchanges between staff and children a consensus is reached about which community feature will be made visible on the new panel. The outcome of some of these exchanges has meant that, over the past eight years, three key features of the community have emerged as being important for the children to add to the Mural.

These were:

♦ a landscape of trees with a stream cascading through them;
♦ a house with trees surrounding it and lightning shooting across the sky;
♦ a tall church steeple with an aeroplane flying overhead.

A tall church steeple with an aeroplane flying overhead

The process identified above was similar, with a few variations, prior to the addition of each of these panels to the Mural. Since each of these was identifying a different feature of the community, what this meant was that a core group of children, who were enthusiastic about this, had to convince their peers that this should be the next panel. This core group became the learning group who led the research and the designing of the panel. However, this did not exclude other children in the nursery from being involved and indeed at different stages in this process they made valuable contributions to its design and development. It was important that this should be so, since because the process of making the panel did stretch very often over two years then some of the children who led the project could leave the nursery for school and others would be left to complete it. This inclusive approach to a project has become key to all the work in this setting and elsewhere and at times, with this and other projects, all the children at some point have become involved. When this happens there is a buzz about the setting that is exhilarating and that we feel is born of a shared purpose and commitment to making something really creative happen.

While this project was about integrating another image of the local community into the Mural it was also about researching why these particular features of the community had such an appeal to this group of children. This became clearer when such questions arose as 'how is it possible to build such a high steeple?', 'why can aeroplanes fly so high above the steeple?' and, interestingly, 'what happens if the aeroplane crashes into the steeple?'. These and other questions generated a great deal of research and discourse with children in the first instance offering their ideas and theories around these particular lines of enquiry. The design and development of this particular panel meant not only revisiting the site where it was originally seen but also capturing the church steeple with the camera, and having the image of the aeroplane to envision scale and size of both in relation to the other panels on the Mural. Such considerations as these ran parallel with other lines of enquiry and what also emerged was the children's interest in the actual stones used in the mosaic of the Mural and another project called the Snake Project. What has been of particular interest to the children in this panel and in the panel currently in progress (The Cherry Tree) is the kind of stones used in the mosaic of the Mural. This has led them to have a keen interest in the different kinds of stones possible to be used in creating a mosaic panel. Some children have been fascinated by the glitter and sparkle of the stones used and others by the different colours of stones chosen by other children in their panel creations. This has been the source of much discussion and caused the children developing this panel to realise that stones were very interesting in themselves and that the range of them meant they had real choices to make in the creation of the background to the panel and the steeple and the aeroplane. They also liked the idea that within one panel a variety of colours and textures of stones could be used. Red for the aeroplane was a unanimous decision and made it stand out against the neutrality of other colours used on the panel. What was also happening throughout this project was the deep enjoyment the children experienced in working with the stones in relation to the touch and feel element that they had access to. The actual sticking of the stones on to the panel led them, as with the original group of children, to discover how this could happen, and much research went into the different types of adhesives that were available and that it was important to know which one to use for specific materials and objects. Again, there was a lot of experimenting to find the adhesive that would work with these stones since it could not be taken for granted that what worked for previous children would be successful for them because the different textures and substance of stones often called for different solutions.

Once all the researching on the various topics that arose throughout this project had been explored, and new understandings reached by children and staff teams, the new panel for the Mural was completed. As previously, the joiner arrived to put it on

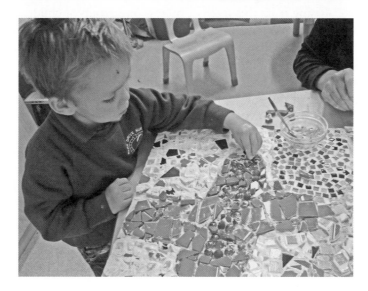

the outside wall and there were great celebrations not only because it represented the community in a much more realistic sense but because of the joy that the children experienced in creating it and the new understandings that they had reached in the process.

Unfortunately, as several years have passed since this was completed, this section of the Mural now needs to be refurbished. The aeroplane has been particularly affected by the weather and Corrie, who was its principal designer, is now aged nine and in the local primary school. His younger sibling is currently at the nursery; Corrie often comes into the nursery with his parents and he has been approached about his willingness to be involved in giving the aeroplane a facelift. He has agreed to this and negotiations are underway between his parents, the nursery and the local primary school as to when this can happen. We like this continuity of involvement of the children when they have left the early years setting, and from our experience the children enjoy making contact again, reminiscing about memorable moments in their life in the early years setting, particularly when that memory is endorsed with a visibility as powerful as the Mural.

Another panel: work in progress: the cherry tree

The creation of this panel has undergone a slightly different process to the others since it has in part been a provocation by the staff team together with the children themselves. The cherry tree had been part of the nursery garden and in late spring it had the most beautiful pink blossom. It had been the subject of much admiration by the children and staff in the setting over a number of years, but sadly it became a casualty of a bad winter a couple of years ago. Staff and children arrived one morning to find that half of the tree had fallen. This created a surge of emotion among staff and children, particularly as they all watched the tree being cut down and reduced to bark chipping for safety reasons. While there was an outpouring of grief there were a lot questions that the children were trying to find answers to in relation to the tree's tragic demise. It was explained to them as part of these conversations that a possible explanation was that water had seeped into the bark, had frozen in the bitterly cold weather and had split the bark of the tree. However, the children liked also to speculate on their own theories that ranged from the wind to giant monsters or dinosaurs stepping on the tree. Arising from this intense interest one group of children in particular felt that they would like to immortalise the tree by creating a panel of it for the Mural. This group of children only had time to start the process of discussion and design of the panel before they left the nursery for school. Before they left they engaged in a great deal of research around trees, such as why this tree only wore its beautiful pink dress at certain times of the year, which caused them to wonder about the seasonal nature of some trees and their many sensory features. The fact that they had left did not quench the desire of the staff team to insert the panel of this beautiful tree, even though many of the children who subsequently attended the nursery had no memory of it. To accommodate both these factors the staff wrote a story about the tree and provided this as a provocation for the children currently in the setting. This provided a lead into a new panel being created; it also, if you like, formed an artificial attachment to the tree as well as an empathy for the children who had been so sad to lose it, but who had been unable to complete the panel that would commemorate it. Again it is important to stress that this has only been possible because a group of children sustained an interest in the tree and the panel once the story had been presented to

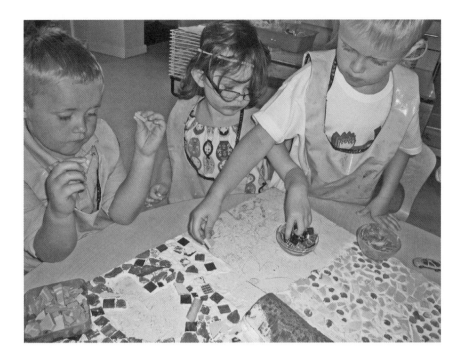

them. This panel is now nearing completion and the children are taking great pride in completing this important task on behalf of the children who experienced this loss. Involvement in creating this panel could well serve as a provocation for these children to create another panel, this time of their own choosing. Time will tell!

This is our current update eight years on; at first glance this could be seen as a product-based project, and there is that outcome element to it, but the democratic process and research that accompanies it is clearly fundamental to each panel that has been created and inserted. At the same time we continue to be intrigued by the ability of the Mural to capture the imagination and enthusiasm of generations of children coming into Park Drive Nursery. Through it, a bond and connection has been made visible, which will always serve as a memory not only of their local community but also of their friends and staff who shared their lives with them in this early years setting.

Notes

1 Buddies are children from Primary 6 in the school within which the nursery is situated. They visit the nursery on a regular basis to make relationships with those children who are going to school in the next school session. This supports these children in their settling-in process when they start school.
2 'Children's meetings' refers to regular meetings that children have within the setting about a range of topics. These can be called by staff or children and are usually around issues that arise within the setting which require discussion and agreement between children and staff.
3 The Play Services team is part of the Early Childhood and Out of School Care Service in Stirling Council.

Chapter 4

Reaching new understandings

The documentation-in-action section in the previous chapter demonstrates our current understanding of the key features of a documentation approach to early learning. In this chapter, it is our intention to share how its implementation is currently impacting on:

◆ children
◆ parents and families
◆ educators and early years staff teams
◆ communities
◆ policy (local and national)

as well as the challenges which are implicit in its adoption as a pedagogical approach.

Children

More visible

Children are more visible. Their learning is being made more visible through photographs, dialogue and the visual presentations of the process and outcomes of documenting children's learning. This includes images and transcripts of children and adults as collaborators in learning which are made available on walls inside and outside, in folders and on laptops and slideshows. These presentations of children working and learning together on episodes and projects in learning groups mean that their voices, views and understandings as people are more visible.

Recently, in Park Drive Nursery, the staff witnessed an example of a child making his capabilities visible in a way which was unexpected. A project was in progress with a core learning group of six children. This project was provoked by a beautiful wall hanging which had been introduced by one of the members of the staff team. As part of their research into making a wall hanging of their own, children and the educator were collaborating on an element of it which meant that at one point, the educator was juggling between two media forms, script and camera, when Max, one of the learning-group members, recognised the educator's dilemma. He said to her, 'Let me have the camera and take the photographs.' She agreed, and since then, Max has become known as the learning-group cameraman who, in this role, recently, when a group of parents was being updated on the projects, was invited to take a photograph. This he did very competently and comfortably, and the outcome was two photographs which served as an important visual record of the meeting.

Increased confidence

Early educators have reported that children are more confident in expressing their views and ideas, that they are more 'outgoing', more readily able to share their thinking on a wide range of topics, both in individual and group situations. On account of this, they have become more able to become involved with the consultation and democratic processes in a much more individual way and are tending to present their own views instead of repeating the response that the child next to them gives. The consequences of consultation processes begin to make more sense to them, even though they struggle, at times, with the concept that the majority view prevails.

In Thornhill Primary School, the Primary 1 teacher was excited by the new enthusiasm and confidence that the children demonstrated when they came into her class from the nursery. She had commented positively to the nursery staff about what she was learning from the children and how she was keen to establish a closer partnership with the nursery in order to build on the way in which children were learning in nursery, in the primary setting.

The impact of spending time in the nursery with the nursery staff, children and parents had a profound effect on the teacher. Significant changes to the school classroom ethos and organisation meant that the children's learning became more visible. More time was given to talking and listening to the children; opportunities for children to explore and solve problems increased; and the children became more involved in planning and assessing their programmes of work in consultation with the teacher. As the children's confidence continued to increase, along with the teacher's confidence, this led to predicted increases in both the pace and quality of learning in school.

Being listened to

The increased opportunities for children to reflect on and review their achievements and their participation in a wide range of activities have led to many children gaining an increased awareness of their value and worth.

Listening and concentrating

From evidence recorded in early years settings and reports from both early educators and some Primary 1 teachers, it seems that for many of the children involved in this approach, their ability to listen and to concentrate for longer periods has increased. Early educators are reporting that children are concentrating for longer periods of time – for example, on stories, conversations and activities – and that they are more purposefully engaged in areas of interest expressed by them and supported by adults.

Learning from each other

As the light and dark episode (Chapter 3) shows, they are becoming skilled at asking questions, engaging in dialogue with each other and with educators and, essentially, are becoming facilitators in small and large group situations. Children are 'speaking up' more in small and large group activities and in other situations. What is noticeable is that their talents and capabilities are becoming more visible, as, for example, some children recognise they have an expertise and put it at the disposal of staff and children and others, becoming able to take more of a leading role. Where this becomes a dominating rather than a lead role, then staff teams are conscious that discussions need to take place with the children about this and strategies need to be adopted which support all the children to have their say and, importantly, help the child to revert back to the lead role rather than the dominant one.

Children's ability to tune in to other children's moods and feelings means that close connections have been established between the children and demonstrates that they are 'listening' with all their senses, as outlined in the following example from practice.

Sam and Craig

Sam and Craig are two four-year-olds at Doune Nursery. Sam's mother is Brazilian, and he had just returned from his first family holiday in Brazil. Part of the holiday had included going on a safari. Sam was particularly interested in the safari animals, and when he came to the nursery, staff provided opportunities for him to play and work with the safari animals. This conversation was recorded between Sam and Craig as they played together with the safari animals in the nursery.

Sam and Craig play with safari animals

Sam:	This is a herd. They are moving all the way from Alaska to Brazil. They have their heads down so they can hear the big boss.
Craig:	The big boss is that cow in front.
Sam:	This bit is Brazil. Brazil is a very important place. There's lots of grass there and a very important person, another queen. The queen is a mummy jaguar.
Craig:	They need a lot more grass and there isn't much food here.
Sam:	Alaska is very dry. Brazil is hot and wet.
Craig:	Lots of sweet grass.
Sam:	Yes, 'cos of all the rain.
Craig:	It fills the Amazon up.
Sam:	The Amazon is a great big river.
Craig:	Where alligators live.
Sam:	And crocodiles called caymans.
Craig:	I've got an alligator book at home.
Sam:	The Amazon is very long and very deep. It's got lots of piranhas and eels, electric eels. It will take the animals one and another day to get to Brazil.
Craig:	That's two days.
Sam:	Brazil is this big.
Craig:	They need their heads down to punch some little animals.
Sam:	No Craig, that's not it. They are listening to the big boss. These animals have to swim across the river to get to the good grass. Brazil is at the bottom of America, Alaska is at the top. The Amazon is the longest river in America, larger than another river in South America. Water buffaloes live in it.
Craig:	Brazil is a special place.
Sam:	Brazil are going to win the World Cup. My mummy says so.

Relationships and interactions

Opportunities for more detailed dialogue, conversations and commentaries between children, and children and adults, have changed the nature of some relationships and interactions. Some early educators reported that they felt closer to the children, and relationships were becoming deeper in the sense that they were 'tuning in' more to children and trusting each other. They also believed that the impact of 'tuning in' to children meant that the range of activities and experiences being developed and offered in the nursery setting was more relevant to children's interests, and the nature of the engagement between the adult and the child supported closer working relations.

Children were also more willing to share with each other; they were more aware of the needs and feelings of others and would offer their support, food, toys and equipment during group activities.

As children increasingly became more confident in taking the lead and sharing with each other, there was a recognition from adults that there was a shift and change in adult and child power relations, and some early educators felt that they were beginning to release some of their 'adult power' by supporting and encouraging children to take the lead and to share responsibility.

More meaningful connections were being made between home and nursery, which supported children's interests and learning across the contexts of both home and nursery. Early educators, parents and families talked about children's increased enthusiasm in sharing and expanding their interests and learning at home.

At a link meeting with a very young parent in Castleview Nursery in a regeneration area of Stirling, early educators were sharing her son's special book with her, which documented visually, through photographs and dialogue, his development and life in the nursery. Sean was two, and the parent was amazed at what this record revealed about him, to the extent that she made a request to take the book home and share it with her immediate and extended family. Having done this, staff suggested that she should take the nursery camera home to record aspects of Sean's development there and also to take photographs of other members of the family. Mum was very enthusiastic about this family involvement, and once the photographs had been returned, the connections between learning at home and the nursery were visibly made on panels on the nursery walls alongside photographs of family members close to Sean. This proved to be a significant breakthrough with this very young parent, and such has been its impact on her and her family that her husband is also about to become involved in the nursery using practical skills that he has to enhance the nursery environment.

Parents and families

Increased involvement

Parents, families and early educators reported that as a result of working with the documentation approach, parents and families become more involved and interested in their children's learning. Parents and families were more actively sharing experiences from home with early educators and were more open to becoming involved in learning-group episodes, projects and events. There was also an increased awareness of the relevance of families sharing responsibility for their children's early learning with early educators, particularly as interests of the children were emerging and revealed a real connection to interests from home. (See Chapter 3, in particular 'One-Eyed Rabbit' and 'Bannockburn Mural'.)

More informed and more confident about their children's learning and development

Parents and families were being given increased evidence of what and how their children were learning and the impact of this learning at home. Parents recorded that they felt more informed about how their children learn. There is also evidence to suggest that some parents, who previously appeared to be less interested in the work of the nursery, had new insights into how the setting operated and, as a result, felt more able to participate. Parents and families also said that they had a better understanding of their own importance and the impact of their relationship and input into their children's learning.

At Arnprior Nursery, the children were involved in a building project which involved them in a great deal of modelling work using areas across the nursery like the building blocks, junk, art and crafts. It became clear as it developed that one of the children had a real talent for making costumes and all the challenges involved with this, whilst another became absorbed with junk modelling techniques. Neither the parents nor the families of these children had understood the extent of their children's capabilities, though they were all delighted to hear about them. Until this time, one of the mums tended to perceive the junk models as just something else to find a place for at home. But, after engaging in conversations with the educator leading on the project, she eventually understood that this is currently an important feature of her child's learning, and she has become much more supportive and interested in his work and life at the nursery and is beginning to see what her role can be in the nursery and at home with her son.

Relationships and interactions

Parents and families reported that they were talking more to their children. As children became more vocal at home and shared their views, ideas and thinking more openly, parents said that they were amazed at their children's capabilities. One parent recorded feeling 'very proud' of her child. Educators recorded that some families appeared to have more understanding and respect when involved with all the children in the nursery, and, as outlined previously, parents were engaging more in their children's interests at home. The following was recorded during an interview with a parent:

> You never have any idea what is happening when you send your child to nursery. You drop them off and you pick them up. This approach means that you can really see what happens in between. You realise just how much your child is contributing to learning in the nursery, and I am reassured. I feel my child is in an environment that will help her to develop . . . a good strong learning environment where her opinion matters, what she has to say matters, and what I say and think matters too . . . this means more to me as a mum, to know all of this.
>
> (Parent, Doune Nursery)

However, it is important to note alongside this that some parents also have reservations, for example, the parents who feel that this democratic process of listening to children through consultation processes is too soon for their child at four years old. They are concerned because they believe that their children are not yet ready to understand fully the nature of the consultation process. They can form this view because sometimes one or two children can become upset because their consultation option was not acted upon because the majority of the children preferred a different option. This has been a critical topic of discussion with some parents and one that we feel may continue to be so. To some extent, the acceptance that children can understand such democratic processes can hinge on an overall belief by adults that children are capable, resourceful and serious in their considerations of a whole range of issues that sometimes they can be excluded from.

Educators and early years staff teams

There has been a profound effect on early educators working with the documentation approach. A real understanding of the endless possibilities of working in this way with children is being recognised. In particular, early educators have developed in the following ways.

Deeper insights

They have deeper insights and understandings and increased awareness of how and what children are learning, children's interests, talents and abilities, how to listen to children and to value listening.

Educators are learning more about how children learn, and although they report feeling more informed about early learning, they also wish to continue to learn, and a new enthusiasm for learning has evolved.

Working more closely together

Early years staff teams have become more sensitive to each other's needs and are working more closely together by sharing understandings, ideas and practice and engaging more in a discourse about children's learning. The increased level and quality of dialogue within staff teams has resulted in more effective team-working as evidenced in 'One-Eyed Rabbit' and 'Light and Dark' (see Chapter 3). However, what is recognised by all involved with this pedagogical approach is the need to be continually upgrading our communication and listening skills, particularly in asking appropriate questions to children and listening to their responses so that scaffolding their learning becomes more possible and more effective.

Tuning in

There is a real desire to be more 'tuned in' to children, to hear more clearly what children are saying and to record and to capture the essence of children's potential through improved observation and reflection techniques. This is allowing early educators to make more sense of what they have understood, both individually and collectively, which impacts significantly on how they support children's early learning.

Recently, in Fallin Nursery, a zero-to-five-years early years setting, one of the educators realised, through her close observations of one of the children in her key group, that he had developed an absorption with the wooden building blocks. This involved him, over a period of several days, in building a series of constructions which were approximating to varying types of shelters or houses. Once the constructions were built, he brought them crashing down as he struggled to put 'house-building' theories into practice. His key person encouraged him to continue despite the considerable noise being created, and she alerted other members of the team to do likewise: this because she understood that there was something really significant in the 'house-building' for this child and, on delving into his family circumstances, realised that his current home circumstances were neither stable nor consistent. The 'house-building', therefore, could well have been a way of him trying to make sense of his situation, and the staff team between them ensured that this opportunity continued to exist for him as long as he needed to play out these scenarios.

What they also realised, through professional dialogue and individual and collective reflections, was that previously they would not necessarily have 'tuned in' to why the child was so interested in 'house-building', and they may well have been inclined to stop the noise rather than find reasons why this was being created in the way that it was. For them, going deeper into this situation had helped them to recognise the importance of really listening to children and pondering on why particular interests arose and then seeking ways in which these could be developed, supported and extended.

Relationships have changed

Relationships and interactions between educators and with children have changed as a result of working with the documentation approach. There has been a greater awareness of the importance of quality interactions with children; more thought is being given to interactions that will extend learning and provide space for thinking (see Chapter 3, 'Pakistan Earthquake' and 'Light and Dark'). These include the range and appropriateness of questions and provocations that are posed to both the children and the adults and the concept of developing a 'spirit of enquiry' whereby children, adults and families are encouraged to question, think, work and research together to find solutions.

There is now a greater understanding about the importance of sharing practice and sharing learning between home and nursery.

One head of an early years setting said, 'We think we know, about children, but we don't. We make too many assumptions. We are too busy supporting children into the physical "doing" rather than the process of "thinking".'

Dialogue

Increased dialogue within staff teams and with children has increased understandings about more appropriate choices in supporting children's learning. Children's interests and talents are being recognised and more readily catered for. A range of opportunities that children can be proactive in developing, organising and choosing has increased independence and interdependence and has promoted a shared ownership of the early learning environment.

The increased dialogue has impacted on the potential for more reciprocal relationships and arrangements. This means that there is a growing expectation that children and adults will share in making decisions that affect them. This has become most visible within the learning-group context, where children and adults are constructing, making meaning and learning together.

More professional dialogue is emerging around learning processes, and there is a greater emphasis on professional reading, research and reflection. Dialogue is being understood as another form of listening to children's voices which had not been previously recognised within that context.

Increased confidence

There is increased confidence in trusting children as active learners. Early educators feel more able to trust children to present their theories, to experiment and explore in an ethos and an environment that supports a model of working that is based on research and enquiry. They also feel more able to trust children to lead their own learning and to support a shared approach to extending their learning. There is also a growing understanding and recognition of children's competencies and confidence, particularly with new technologies, as adults witness children's capacities to engage with the range of technology available to support early learning.

New professionalism

A new professionalism is emerging from a growing belief and awareness of the personal qualities, dispositions, skills and competencies of an effective educator. Educators are taking more risks as learners and researchers themselves; they feel more able to share with other professionals and parents, their ideas, thoughts and understandings, which has led to more effective team-working.

Equally, amongst all this ongoing reflection and reconstructing of working practices, there have been some acutely painful examples of staff having a perception that they were, for example, allowing children's interests and ideas to be taken seriously when video footage that has been taken reveals something entirely different.

Such a situation arose in Arnprior Nursery when two members of the staff team were in the initial stages of a project on water. As part of this, the children and the educators were discussing together how they could access a larger container than the water trough which was currently being used for exploration and discovery but was proving to have space limitations. To access a larger space for the water, the staff engaged in a consultation exercise with the children about resource possibilities that existed within the early years settings to accommodate more water. Quite an extended discussion ensued, and, eventually a solution was found to this problem. The interesting element of this was the process of how this came about. The video footage clearly revealed that the staff member who was leading on the consultation with the children was seen to be looking for the children to find the solution which she already felt was the right container for the water before the discussion with the children took place. Despite the many good suggestions that the children made, none of them was acceptable until eventually one child gave the member of staff the response she was looking for.

When she saw the footage, she was embarrassed and pained at what was revealed but was very willing for this to be shared with her own staff team and others in other settings since she realised that this needed to be made widely available so that others could learn from her mistakes. Her misconception of how she handled this was a really important learning curve for her and one that she would not readily forget.

Communities

Increased visibility of the children in the community

This is one of the reported outcomes of working in this way. Although this is still at an early stage, staff are more frequently providing opportunities for children to become involved and to participate in community activities and events and are more likely to build in and include elements of community engagement in their projects. In one nursery, the children were taking pictures of local buildings, and, as they were doing this, they naturally began to tell local residents and other community members what they were doing. The impact of this was that the wider local community began to join in and take an interest in what the children were doing. One local resident commented on the fact that 'he wished he could use a digital camera.' The following week, he called in to the nursery to tell the teacher that he had been so inspired by the children that he had signed up for classes on how to use a digital camera.

Increased involvement of the wider community in the work of the nursery

The increased confidence of the staff and the visibility of the children's learning in the home and in the community has encouraged and promoted greater awareness and understanding locally of the work of the nursery and how and what children are learning, evidenced in the example of the Bannockburn Mural in Chapter 3. Early years educators report enthusiastically on the interest shown by local community members and of the many offers to become involved in projects and nursery developments.

Though this is still at an early stage, members of the local community have also become more visible in the work of the nursery as their images, dialogue and involvement are recorded and documented in presentations featured around the nursery. Where this is happening, we can see that adult views of what and how children learn and the importance of children's early learning is beginning to change.

For example, specialists from the wider community are photographed working alongside the children as they were at Croftamie Nursery during the course of an outside project which involved the children in making toadstool seats alongside a sculptor. A similar visible profile was given to the dog-rescue specialist at Fintry Nursery when she came in with one of the dogs to talk and discuss the dog's disabilities with the children. On both of these occasions, the specialists from the community not only entered into a dialogue with the staff about how to work with young children in these situations but were also impressed by the ability of the children to have practical involvement in the experience and to be able to frame really insightful questions about the tasks and topics under discussion.

Policy

Local

The impact of working with the documentation approach has had a significant impact on local policy, thinking and development. The enthusiasm, insights and desire to share outcomes and understandings with all early educators and others was most compelling and led to the production of the 'Working with Documentation' guide aimed at all early years staff across the Stirling Council area. The guidance set out our current thinking about the documentation approach and a framework that would support early years educators to explore the approach in practice within their own settings.

The importance of staff development has also been recognised, and a comprehensive programme was devised to support working with documentation in practice. The content of the programme explored and explained theories and principles underpinning the documentation approach and included practical examples of the approach in action. The programme also encouraged professional dialogue and strategies that would promote professional discourse and collaboration between early educators both within and across settings. It also encouraged reflection and provided access to professional reading materials. The delivery of the programme was both course- and practice-based, with support for individual settings. Local networks were also established to support settings to work together in the putting of the documentation approach into practice.

In order to assess the impact of the staff-development programme, outcomes were recorded and an action research model established by an external researcher.[1] The outcomes and key findings from this have been integrated into this publication.

The implications of our new understandings around documentation and our approach to staff development means that, in general, the application of the core elements of the documentation approach is built in and embedded in all local staff-development programmes.

We have been very privileged to be working with others on this approach and, in particular, with Carlina Rinaldi, Pedagogical Consultant to Reggio Children, who has been guiding us, sharing with us and challenging us with her perspective and understandings on this way of working, thinking and living. As a result, we have devised a 'project' with Carlina which is encouraging us to develop our thinking and our approach in Stirling and to see this as an 'encounter'. As a result, we have begun to review our current methods and to change our approach to how we develop policy and practice. This included establishing the Stirling Documentation Group, which aims to:

◆   lead and research the documentation approach in Stirling;
◆   consider and make explicit our understandings about documentation in order to reach a shared understanding;
◆   devise key strategic and operational objectives for the implementation of a documentation approach to early learning in Stirling and possibly further afield.

National

There has been growing interest nationally to find out more about the ways in which we are working with documentation. Other local authorities, individual settings and some national organisations and agencies, such as Learning and Teaching Scotland and Learning Unlimited and Children in Scotland, are keen to hear more about:

◆   the impact of listening to children;
◆   our views and understandings about the image of children as rich and resourceful;
◆   documentation as a tool in making learning visible.

Following a major review of the current curriculum arrangements for children in early years and schools, a new national curriculum framework for children aged three to eighteen years has been devised in Scotland. The new curriculum framework represents our developing understanding about the ways in which children learn and our aspirations for all Scotland's children to be successful learners, confident individuals, responsible citizens and effective contributors. At the core of this framework, the values and principles of documentation are clearly represented. This includes children's rights, responsibilities, respect, participation and an image of children as active social agents with rich capabilities. This new framework and the support materials have the potential to assist the core elements of the documentation approach to be embedded in practice across all early years settings in Scotland.

This is supported further by cross-cutting themes within the curriculum for excellence such as citizenship and democracy, which recognises children as citizens now rather than in waiting.

The contribution from Stirling has been recognised in these key national policies.

Challenges

Cultural

From the work and research we are engaged in, we have come to understand that there are many challenges to working in this way. Working with the documentation approach is not easy, and, at times, there can be real tensions. People do not always agree or share the same perspectives, and we have found that some colleagues feel unhappy with this potential conflict of views and perspectives. Working successfully with the documentation approach means that educators must be willing to enter into professional dialogue, and, for some, this can be uncomfortable. Early years staff teams may be at different stages in their understanding; some educators find that they have more understanding and skills to engage in this particular way of working than others. Those who do not feel so confident can feel anxious about 'getting it right' and that they need to be working to the 'right answer'. This cultural shift brings with it uncertainty, and although uncertainty can be viewed as a value, for some educators this can be unnerving. For example, there is no 'set way or tick list' of ready-made questions or responses to assist staff in the best way of taking a conversation forward. (This is illustrated in Chapter 3 in the conversation between the Head, James and Fergus in 'Pakistan Earthquake'.)

Professional development

How best to support people involved in the documentation approach who are at different levels of understanding is one of the major challenges facing the service and individual settings. As set out earlier in this chapter, we have engaged in a comprehensive and successful programme to support staff in such a way that builds on their enthusiasm and openness to learn. We have developed learning networks, encouraged joint research and provided dedicated staff-development days. All early years staff have five in-service/professional development days built into their core working conditions.

Sustaining and developing an effective model of staff training and development remains a key priority. We are currently giving consideration to the best way to develop resources and materials that will offer continuous support. Staff teams seem to prefer a mixture of ongoing training sessions combined with critical enquiry sessions, both within their own settings and in collaboration with others. Currently, these benefit from being led by a key person who can pose significant questions around the pieces of documentation being presented. What remains problematic is the differentiation and sustainability elements, since some settings have been working on this approach for five years whilst others have been involved for only two. The hope would be to get those who have been involved longest to be able to take more of a lead role in supporting others who are newer to the approach. This would clearly have the advantage of tackling both of these identified problems. However, in the meantime, the intention is to develop a range of resources and materials to support staff teams in specific areas which they are identifying as 'sticking points', such as how to identify children's key interests and how to record a learning process and its key stages. What forms of enquiry will help us to find this out? An important element of any professional development strategy is access to professional reading, which continues to be supported by a central lending system, and there is an expectation that professional dialogue will be generated as a result of this.

We continue to discuss and consider other ways of developing our professional development programme, which supports staff teams in their implementation of this approach, both in terms of content, design and time.

Time

Managers and heads of early years settings view time as one of the major challenges facing them in working with this approach. They feel it is difficult to find enough time to talk, time to listen, time to reflect, time to record and time to be together. We have come to believe that changing our understanding and philosophy of what we mean by time, seeing it more as a value and changing our perspective on what we think is our core activity in relation to time is an ongoing challenge.

Our construct on time can be seen as a reflection on current society where everything seems to be pressurised and we are all trying to fit too many things into any one twenty-four-hour day. Nurseries can be like this too. One of the issues around time that we seem to be grappling with in early childhood settings is what do we give our time to? One response could be that time should be given to listening to children, trying to interpret their interests and understandings, making observation visible and slowing down the pace and embedding the elements of the documentation approach into everyday practice. This could also include recording alongside children, getting their view on a situation or image which is in the process of being recorded so that the process being captured within a learning group or of an individual child can be recorded at the time that it is happening. There is a growing recognition that staff teams need to be more creative and resourceful in how best to allocate time. Going at a slower pace will be helpful to children as well as to staff teams since many children are part of a rushed environment in the rest of their lives and will perhaps appreciate the ability to live their nursery lives in the slow rather than the fast lane. It is not being suggested that 'it should be a contest between speed and slowness, but about having the courage to rediscover the time of human beings' (Rinaldi, personal communication, 2005).

Ethics

> We always have to pose questions concerning what right we have to interpret and document children's doings and what is ethically legitimate.
>
> (Dahlberg et al. 1999: 156)

Working with documentation has encouraged us to think more deeply about the concept of ethics and, in particular, about ethical practice and what this means. This has come about as a result of working outside traditional approaches and a dominant discourse. When there is no one or 'right' answer or pre-defined outcome, faced with choices, the question of responsibility is raised and, with it, the balance of rights and responsibilities.

Although we are witnessing a change in relationships with children, we are still acutely aware of the issues around the balance of power and are in the early stages of exploring what we understand by ethical relationships. We are now asking the following questions:

◆ Do we have the consent of children to record and interpret their thoughts?
◆ How effectively are we listening to all of our children?
◆ Are we only listening to those who have the most to say or those who are the most skilled at telling us?

◆ Are children with additional needs included in the projects and do they have visibility?

We have no 'one' answer. We have come to realise that there are many ways of thinking about and comprehending the meaning of ethical practice, and we are at an early stage in exploring and engaging in dialogue with staff teams on reaching new understandings about this.

Transition and continuity of learning from nursery into primary school

The impact of working with the documentation approach in early years is beginning to be felt in the early stages of primary. Some primary teachers are beginning to comment on the differences that they see in the children, in particular, the increased confidence of children to share ideas and views and to participate actively in their learning. Some primary teachers are amazed at the richness and resourcefulness of children and are excited about the possibilities. In a small number of primary-school settings, Primary 1 teachers are beginning to explore new ways in which they can work with elements of the documentation approach in the classroom. Although there is an increasing interest and evidence of change in developing and engaging in more active and participatory approaches in the early stages of primary, there continues to be a number of early years teachers in primary schools who are resistant and find this way of working and the confidence of the children threatening and against their perceived order. It is not uncommon for some primary teachers to 'complain' to the nursery heads and staff team that the children coming from the nursery are 'too assertive' and challenging.

As a result of this, we have embarked on a transition programme and framework that involves early years and primary staff, parents and families to support both the continuity of learning and approaches to learning from home to nursery and nursery into Primary 1. In addition, one or two early years settings are using a current documentation project as a subject of transition which continues into Primary 1 (reception class). In another, the staff are making a presentation of their project to the Primary 1 teacher in a local primary school prior to the children's entry there. They will do this accompanied by the children, parents and families who were involved in it. It is their hope that this will serve a double purpose: first, that the staff working with children going into Primary 1 (reception class) will have a better understanding of the children's capabilities, and, second, it will help them to recognise the potential of documentation for making visible the children's learning and their progress. The main challenges facing the services and the settings are the differences in culture, staff–child ratios and the impact of the national curriculum, although, in Scotland, we are now implementing a national three-to-eighteen curriculum that specifically states that the approaches to early learning should be visible in the early stages primary. This work is ongoing.

Note

1   External Action Research Project – staff development.

Chapter 5

Reflections, and what next?

Reflections

We realised that it was important to develop an approach which was complementary to our own existing values and principles. What it caused us to do midway through our process was to revisit these and fully understand their importance in promoting and developing this pedagogical approach across a whole council area. Our challenges would have been even greater if we had to negotiate a new set of values and principles and, at the same time, adopt a new approach to children's learning as well. Our existing values and principles gave us a sound foundation on which to build the documentation approach to early learning. It is also clear to us now, despite real doubts that we have had from time to time, that to pilot this approach with just five nurseries in the beginning on a trial-and-error basis was probably an important decision since we were all in at the deep end and had to support each other's understandings as we went along. Interestingly, we have since learned that these nurseries did not quite believe that those of us who were leading on this approach were learning alongside them, even though we had shared this with them. We think they probably felt reassured by disbelieving us at this point!

The impact of adopting this approach has been significant in helping us to understand:

◆ what listening to children really means (we thought we were doing this already);
◆ how important the process of shared observations is in looking and actually seeing what is happening even with very young children;
◆ how rich and resourceful young children really are in their ability to pose problems and solve problems and to be researchers and theorists alongside adults;
◆ how the visibility of this approach has been able to draw families into the learning processes of their child in a way that has not been contrived or 'set up';
◆ how thoughtful educators have become about their own practice;
◆ how they are becoming more able to identify their own learning needs alongside those of the children.

Further, it has led some of us to recognise the importance of space indoors and outdoors in the documentation process:

◆ space for children to explore;
◆ space for them to be together in a learning group or on their own;
◆ space to think and consider options to current problems;
◆ space that is organised to make space not simply to house resources;
◆ space that makes visible the documentation approach to early learning.

Some of the emerging realisations have been that staff feel that they could not go back to 'being' with children in the way that they previously were. Whilst it is still possible for them to revert back to previous ways when they are confronted with the uncertainty that this approach can generate, at some level they understand that this is only a brief respite, for, deep down, they know that they are getting a much better sense of the child through pedagogical documentation. For some staff, at times, this has become an incredible experience, and this is evident in the way that they present a panel of documentation for discussion and comment. They cannot quite believe what they are discovering about the children because it is overturning all 'previous knowns' that they have been working within, and, still further, they cannot believe that they are able to uncover such amazing capabilities in the children, which they will honestly say they would not have noticed or known in their previous way of interacting with the children.

Other realisations have been that, being part of a professional dialogue forum, all of us have learned something else from each other, either about ourselves, the children and families or about the documentation process itself. Nobody is exempt from the process. We are finding such encounters have the capability both to scare and inspire us, such can be the depth, discomfort and exhilaration that can be felt in gaining understandings of this approach and what it can mean now and in the future for children, families and educators.

Democracy and citizenship

What has also become clear to us is that all the strands of the documentation approach, such as consultation, listening to children's many voices, learning in groups and recognising the importance of hearing what other people have to contribute and are good at, are all elements of a democratic society. Therefore, children engaged with this approach are living the democratic process in their daily lives at the nursery. (See Chapter 3, 'One-Eyed-Rabbit', children's meetings.)

The fact that children are citizens from birth means that they are living their entitlement within the early years setting. What we have understood more deeply is what an important role the documentation approach has to play in accustoming young children to the democratic process. This is an important civic role that each early years setting is embracing and one that staff teams, when confronted with it, can feel over-whelmed by. They sometimes find it difficult to recognise what a potentially important role they are playing in society since there is a tendency to see their work in the early years setting as important work but to some extent separate from society and certainly not extending into the realms of civic society.

> Through making pedagogical work both visible and a subject for democratic and open debate, pedagogical documentation provides a possibility for early childhood institutions gaining a new legitimacy in society.
>
> (Dahlberg *et al.* 1999: 145)

One of the issues can be that in our culture children are not necessarily taken seriously and are often referred to as citizens in waiting, further casting them in 'the becoming' role rather than as citizens now. Talking to parents and families about this perspective of the documentation approach can sometimes be tricky because they do not recognise what important ideas and opinions their children have, and the visibility of this approach, which demonstrates their children's capabilities, can be helpful in this regard. However, we recognise that we have to continue to have conversations with staff, families and other professionals about the important implications of this approach for children now and in the future.

What next?

Where we go from here is something that all of us continue to be thoughtful about. What feels right at this time is that our priorities must be around finding differentiated ways in which to support staff teams, to continue to develop our critical thinking skills and to become more able to engage professionally when hard discussions arise which take us to hard places and can make us feel uncomfortable.

It seems imperative that we develop a much better understanding of the difference between episodes and projects and their respective importances in the documentation process. We must become more courageous and construct ways together which help us to make professional decisions about when an interest of a child or children has the learning potential to become a project. We must not overlook either the necessity to continue to document individual interests that children have which do not become either a project or an episode but also deserve to be documented and made visible in the same way as projects.

The essentiality of the learning-group culture within this approach and its ability to be transformational to the learning, teaching and development of all children cannot be underestimated, particularly when it is seen at first hand; our ability to support it and to find ways of integrating it into the life of the setting remains a crucial factor in progressing this pedagogical approach further.

The presentation of this approach must be more appropriately articulated to others so that their understanding of its crucial elements is clear. All of us need to become less self-conscious about 'having a go' and letting go of the 'getting it right' agenda.

We also recognise and are working hard at continuing this approach into Primary 1 (reception class) in the primary school so that core elements of this pedagogical approach will become embedded in the thinking and practice of the early years settings within the primary school. A pilot is being embarked upon currently, but we realise that this will be a very gradual process which will need a similar kind of support that nursery staff have had access to since the outset of the implementation of the documentation approach. This is clearly important for the continuity and progression of learning, which remains one of our key aims since children going into primary school will adapt much more quickly to a new setting if the attitudes and practices of the staff teams are similar to those encountered in the early years nursery setting.

All of our work with children aged three to five has inevitably raised the question, what about children under three? It is not only a question that we ask of ourselves but also one that is asked of us frequently by any group that is seeking to know more about this pedagogical approach. We have understood this as a necessary next step in our process, and, informally, we have already started to introduce it in those settings where children under three attend. What is becoming clear to us is that we may need to construct ways of doing this which could be different from those currently adopted with the older children. At this very early stage, staff are working on this and are already finding that their early documentation is revealing how this approach with the younger children is allowing them access to their interests, how they learn and their relationships with other children. None more so than with those children who have not yet included verbal language in their range of communications.

Below, we have included one of our initial attempts at documentation with children under three. What this represents is a glimpse of what is possible with this age group through the documentation approach to early learning.

Context

Castleview Nursery is an extended day nursery for children in the three-months-to-five-years age group in a regeneration area of Stirling. The pattern of attendance is both full- and part-time, and the catchment area is quite mixed, accommodating mostly an urban population of children and their families.

How did it start?

It started with the staff team observing the children to confirm a view that they had that some of the children were showing a keen interest in technology. The outcome was that two or three children were sustaining an interest in cameras and the computer. The interests and the learning processes of the three children were documented, and one of these children in particular was seen as being of great significance, particularly as she was a child who did not yet speak English (neither did her parents, Mandarin being their first language).

The two children in this episode are Shihan, two years and two months, and Marie, one year and eight months.

What staff had realised, through their ongoing observations, was that Shihan had seemed to make a really important connection with Marie, who was a child who had been in and out of hospital with a heart condition.

Alongside this important attachment, Shihan had been demonstrating, over a period of time, a keen interest in the digital camera and had spent a lot of time examining and experimenting with it.

During her exploration of the camera, one of the aspects she had really enjoyed was watching the images on the screen after she had been taking photographs. Her first successful photograph was, not unexpectedly, of Marie. She was very pleased with the outcome, and staff observed her giving a secret smile. Staff reporting on this felt that since she could not tell Marie in words that she was her friend that the camera had become her voice.

Since staff were very aware of Shihan's developing friendship with Marie and also her fascination with the digital camera, they supported both children in this relationship and Shihan with her interest in the camera.

The relationship between Shihan and Marie continued and, one day, two amazing events occurred. On account of Marie's health difficulties, she had not reached usual milestones and was experimenting with the process of becoming mobile. Within the setting at this time, both children and staff lived in a state of high expectation that

Marie would express her mobility soon. The day when she eventually made the movement of raising herself to her feet, Shihan went for the camera and captured this momentous event through it. Staff wondered if she understood the importance of this 'happening' and made it visible or if her main interest was the camera.

Importantly, also, the staff noticed what Shihan was doing and its significance for her, and photographed Shihan photographing Marie.

When Shihan's mother next came into the nursery, through the photographs, the staff were able to share with her what Shihan had been able to achieve. Mum then tried to explain that they had a camera at home and that she would bring it in the

Shihan has shown an interest in the digital camera.

she spent lots of time, looking and inspecting it, turning it over and experimenting with the buttons.

Shihan found the button that controls the zoom lens. She spent lots of time looking at the images on the screen.

Shihan and digital camera

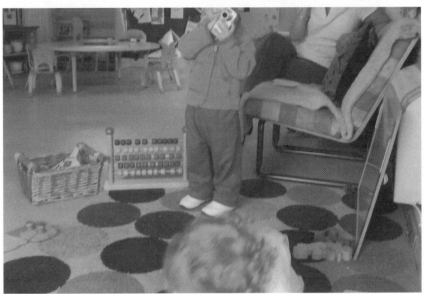

Shihan and Marie

next day with her relative who spoke some English. This she did, and the camera became a really important way of involving Mum in the nursery, which was particularly helpful since Shihan's younger sister was about to be admitted to the nursery.

Mum used her camera in the nursery and made an important home–nursery link as well as a way of communicating with the nursery.

This episode is ongoing and already has changed in terms of other happenings within the nursery and the admission to the nursery of Shihan's younger sister. What is self-evident is the importance of implementing this pedagogical approach with very young children. Constructing ways of doing this has become a high priority for us, and what has been shared here is one way which already looks different in its

Shihan and Marie on the floor

Shihan's mum taking picture

Shihan and Marie on the floor

presentation and application to how we document the learning processes for three-to five-year-old children.

We thank the reader for accompanying us on the journey so far and hope it has inspired you to adopt the documentation approach to early learning within your own setting. We look forward to meeting up with you again in our next publication when we will make visible our next encounter with the documentation approach to early learning with children under three years of age.

Eight years on . . . Shihan: the spaces in between

by Fiona Russell and Delia Binney

> Stories are powerful research tools. They provide us with a picture of real people in real situations, struggling with real problems.
>
> (Witherall and Noddings 1991: 280)

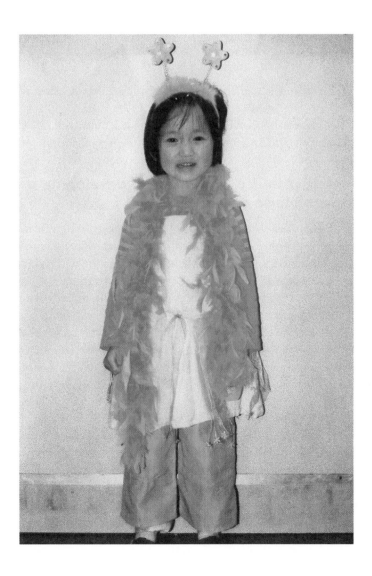

Our reason for updating Shihan's story is because she presented us with a series of questions that remained unanswered when we last parted company with her in the first edition (see p. 73). You may recall that Shihan's first language was not English, so throughout our first narration of her story we were deeply into making assumptions about her through observations and relationships she made, notably with Marie, a child with additional support needs, in the nursery and with the camera. She and her family intrigued the staff team and anybody who was familiar with her life in the nursery.

This intrigue has continued up to the present day and because of this it was decided to chart Shihan's progress over the last eight years in nursery and in the primary school that she now attends. This has been made easier since it is on the same campus as the nursery and there are meaningful contacts between both settings. The co-authors of this piece, the key worker and the original researcher, set out not only to track her progress but also to test out the assumptions that they made about Shihan when she was two years old and how this was made more possible through the ongoing implementation of pedagogical documentation.

This was an extensive piece of research and we have decided to highlight those aspects that connect most closely with those raised when we first met her in the first edition.

At that time our questions were:

◆ Is Shihan's interest in the camera or in developing a relationship with Marie and others?
◆ What was dispositional and what was Shihan's learning style?
◆ How will pedagogical documentation make visible her development and learning?

Is Shihan's interest in the camera or in developing a relationship with Marie and others?

Shihan's use of the camera to record Marie's progress at a significant point in her learning became a focal point for staff in trying to work out what this could mean. Did it mean that she was trying to establish a relationship with Marie, or was she using the camera as a voice to communicate to the staff team one of her interests and competences? From what subsequently occurred it seems to have been much more about using the camera as a voice rather than making a relationship with Marie. This became increasingly clear with Shihan's continued use of the camera, which she used to forge links between the key worker and the family, in particular her mother.

Shihan's images, along with those the staff took, revealed to Mum how engaged and safe she was in the nursery; this meant that a breakthrough became possible. Prior to this, staff had been trying many different strategies to engage with Mum, especially Fiona, the key worker. These strategies included, for example, being there every day to meet and greet Shihan and her mum, and learning words of Mandarin to have a conversation with Mum, albeit in a limited way. However, the power of Shihan's images they understood were crucial to the establishing of a better relationship with Mum, and they began to use their own documentation to support hers. Together they proved effective allies in revealing to Mum how she belonged to the nursery community. Finding her voice through the camera we believed empowered Shihan and became central to her learning, enabling her to record her achievements when she did not have the oral language to communicate them to the staff team. An example of this was when she had completed a challenging floor puzzle: she immediately went for the camera and took a photograph of it to place in her journal (a personal folder for each child that records her/his learning journey in the nursery). For Shihan, the camera engaged all the key players in relation to her learning and her life. These could either be found in her journal or could have been taken home – whichever she found to be most important for her at the time.

In answer to the question, 'was Shihan using the camera to forge a relationship with Marie?', what we have understood is that this was probably not her main focus. It was a way of connecting with another child and Shihan was able to use the lens of the camera to support her family in connecting and developing relationships with Fiona, her key worker, and other members of the staff team.

Shihan – what was dispositional and what was her learning style?

What pedagogical documentation has made visible is not only what interests Shihan in learning and what she is learning, but also how she is learning. The way she approaches learning and her style of learning has made us think more deeply about how as well as what children learn. This has accessed us to amazing insights and understandings of children, of which our experience with Shihan is just one.

Lillian Katz (1995) states: 'all we are learning about the impressionable young brain indicates that beliefs, attitudes and dispositions are being shaped in infancy'. Katz further differentiates between feelings and dispositions: 'The former are emotional states, while the latter are habits of mind that result in patterns of behaviour. Feelings can be powerful, but with young children can be transitory while dispositions are likely to be more stable and long lasting' (cited in Dowling 2000, p. 68).

Throughout the action research project, Shihan's learning styles were beginning to emerge. During professional discourse with the staff team we began to understand that Shihan:

◆ observed first;
◆ recorded (through use of the camera); and
◆ imitated (using her doll).

She wanted to know how things work. She also demonstrated a keen interest in Marie and how she worked!

With further observation, staff were beginning to understand that Shihan's continual search for knowledge went beyond her use of the camera and her study of Marie. Increasingly, we came to understand that Shihan used her doll to replicate experiences in the nursery that Shihan had first observed Marie doing. The doll was the experimental tool with which Shihan made sense of her environment while supporting her learning styles. Shihan's dispositions for learning were becoming evident as she demonstrated high levels of motivation, curiosity, problem solving and creativity.

As Shihan's life in the nursery continued, her developing understanding of the world around her was revealed as she demonstrated fascinations for certain aspects of living, for example, she asked 'What is a dream?', 'What does a wedding mean?'. She also made very clear statements about her identity: 'I'm Chinese, not Scottish. My mammy told me.'

At this time staff were aware of how important Shihan's journal was to her and her family. She used it as a link for connecting her life in nursery with that of home. Through her journal, Shihan was able to revisit her learning and to see and talk about her progression in learning as her journey continued from nursery to school. Her family were very proud of Shihan and were able to articulate this through her journal.

Have Shihan's dispositions for learning become habits of mind?

The following gives us a further insight into the above as she moves from the nursery setting into the primary-school setting.

The following is an extract from her Starting Points profile (Starting Points was designed as a working document for all educators working in nursery and Primary 1. Its main purpose was to support reflective educators in the process of gathering information about each child's learning and development: in the curriculum planning process in transition situations, and in supporting the smooth transition from nursery to Primary 1.)

> [Shihan is] a quiet, sensitive, gentle person. She is comfortable and confident in smaller groups. She is self-aware and shows a keen interest in learning. She asks good questions and has great respect for the needs and feelings of others.
>
> She can have quiet times when she seems to be processing all the information, language and stimuli that surround her. She uses very subtle expressions and gestures to communicate.

Here is an example of her using her body language to communicate that she has finished her work and she is happy with the result. She remained silent.

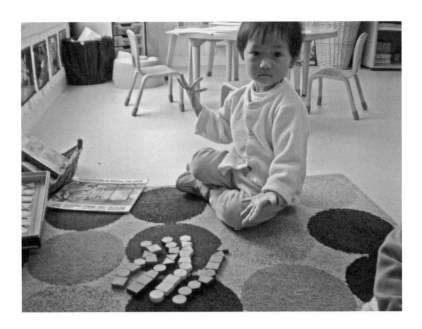

Her profile continues:

> Shihan is a visual learner who prefers to try and test new experiences several times
> (and usually with a prop – her doll or soft toy) to ensure she understands and can
> master the skills needed to complete tasks successfully.

Shihan always organises herself before engaging in new experiences. She gathers
the tools and resources she requires and appears to prepare herself physically and
mentally for learning. She makes her self-discipline and control visible.

During the transition visits to school, her parents were delighted to join her and
give their support to her. The relationships they have with the nursery are now well
established and are based on mutual trust and respect, which continues to deepen as
Shihan's siblings follow in her footsteps.

Has Shihan demonstrated patterns of behaviour as she has progressed through school from Primary 1 to Primary 4?

When reading her school reports it is evident that Shihan's patterns of behaviour are
well established. She is quiet, confident, sensitive to others, conscientious and
hardworking. She is always ready to learn and ready to support others in their learning.

We believe that our hypothesis is correct and that what we observed in nursery is
a true reflection of how Shihan learns. In tracking Shihan we have come to understand
the vital role the documentation approach has had in helping us to understand how
Shihan learns as through this her capabilities have been made visible to us. We have
also come to realise that the dispositions and patterns of behaviour that Shihan revealed
to us in nursery are highly visible in school. Through her journals, profiles and images,
we see Shihan as competent, rich and resourceful.

Here is our supporting evidence:

Other voices

The following are two conversations that tell us more about Shihan as she progresses on her journey.

Conversation with Shihan's class teacher

In recording this interview with the class teacher we are mindful of the difference in contexts where Shihan is now living and learning. While we recognise that there is more formality in the school setting, which incidentally is in a process of change to become more in tune with our early years thinking and practice, the nature of the comments that the teacher makes about Shihan needs to be understood within their context.

The class teacher's view is that Shihan is an observer who is driven to find things out about herself and others. She looks, listens closely and measures her ability against others. She is visually astute, which is evident in the attention to detail she makes visible in her artwork. Shihan always waits for permission from the teacher before she will go ahead. She likes to achieve, deals well with success and hardly ever fails. Shihan is in the top group where she enjoys independent and extended learning, ensuring that the curriculum is differentiated to support her ability. Shihan is very imaginative, which she expresses in her artwork and her story writing. She absorbs all of the storytelling techniques and takes the story line further.

Shihan is empathetic to the needs of others, caring for more vulnerable children. The teacher refers to her as a 'high flyer', who demonstrates a real ability as a scaffolder in learning. She is a good learning buddy and others like working with her. She is self-contained, quiet, calm, measured and supportive. She is very popular and was voted onto the student council by her peers. Shihan is a child who is always ready, always attentive and has an enthusiasm for learning. Shihan's attitude is highly focused and never varies.

Conversation between Shihan and Fiona Russell, researcher and Shihan's key worker, Raploch Nursery

It seemed to us, that tracking Shihan's footsteps would not be complete without hearing her voice about where she is now and what contribution the nursery made to her life and learning. Fiona Russell, during Shihan's time in the nursery, made a really significant relationship with her and with her whole family. She continues to maintain this strong and important contact with the family and Shihan to this day. It therefore was fitting that she should be the person to have this conversation with Shihan.

Shihan finds school fun and she looks forward every day to being at school. She thinks she is good at Art, Maths and Reading and has books at home that she studies. She attends Chinese school and also enjoys her experiences there as she thinks it's important for her to learn in Chinese as well as English. She recognises that her learning style is to figure things out for herself, but she 'listens to instructions'. She says:

> I feel included in school because I was born here, I am half Scottish and half Chinese. I am glad I was born here although it is much warmer in China! I have

lots of friends who come to my house. Mrs Campbell is my favourite teacher because she gives us popcorn parties. I am the leader (first violin) of the Red Orchestra. I am moving to Riconada Orchestra of the Big Noise soon. That's a higher orchestra. Everyone says they want to be in my team in class or gym. That makes me feel lucky.

Fiona asks 'if you hadn't gone to nursery would anything be different?'. Shihan replies, 'I would maybe be more shy. I learned a lot at nursery'.

(Big Noise is a social transformational initiative, founded in Venezuela, which seeks to improve the lives of children, families and communities through music and working in an orchestra. Stirling Council and Sistema Scotland work in partnership to fund this initiative in the regeneration area of Raploch, Stirling.)

How did pedagogical documentation make visible Shihan's development and learning?

Pedagogical documentation has given us a vehicle for understanding how to work more effectively with Shihan. We were able to trace Shihan's journey in a variety of different ways and by employing different tools in the documentation process – for example:

- observations
- respectful interactions
- the nurturing of relationships
- professional discourse
- narratives
- photographs
- dialogue
- a range of media
- journals.

Pedagogical documentation is a powerful lens through which children's learning processes, strategies and dispositions for learning are made visible. It is a collaborative process that involves working closely with parents and other adults who know children well.

Pedagogical documentation: reflection from Fiona Russell, Shihan's key worker

My encounter with pedagogical documentation coincided with Shihan starting her early year's education at Raploch Nursery. It would prove to be a rewarding, at times frustrating, challenging and exciting partnership. I was struggling to understand and adopt this new approach as much as Shihan was struggling with the daily challenges that the unfamiliar nursery environment was presenting to her. Reflecting on Shihan's first months with us I reached an understanding that she was faced with information overload: sensory, cultural and linguistic! I was desperate for Shihan to begin to communicate in a more meaningful way with me. I realise now that she needed time: time to assimilate, make meaning of and process all of the information she was receiving.

Through documentation, using photographs, observation notes and creating her journal together, I was able to reach a deeper understanding of Shihan and the 'Hundred Languages of Children'. As I started to listen with all of my senses, it all began to make sense.

The documentation showed me that Shihan was connecting up experiences and was beginning to make sense of her world, and it became clear that she was constructing and scaffolding her own learning and demonstrating how open she was to the learning opportunities and experiences on offer and how eager she was to learn.

Working with children under the age of three, using the pedagogical documentation approach to learning allowed us to involve parents in their children's learning and make visible each child's progression as well as their learning style. This was a crucial factor in Shihan's case and in those of her siblings who followed her into Raploch Nursery.

Using this approach when working with Shihan and other very young children demonstrates that they are very capable and resourceful people and that they do indeed have 'a hundred languages'.

> Children are people full of ideas and thoughts who are seeking sense and meaning and have much to tell and to show.
>
> (*Traces from Reggio*, Meeuwig, Schepers and van der Werf 2009: 79)

My practice and how I perceive children has been influenced and enhanced by my encounter with pedagogical documentation. My way of working as part of a team has also been influenced as I am confident to challenge and engage in dialogue with colleagues in an effort to share my belief and commitment to this way of working.

It would be important in considering Shihan's story to read and reflect upon the following passage from a chapter by George Forman and Brenda Fyfe entitled 'Negotiated Learning through Design, Documentation, and Discourse' in *The Hundred Languages of Children: The Reggio Emilia Approach – Advanced Reflections* (pp. 245–6):

Documentation, as we mean it here, is more focused on children than on a child. Even when a child is featured in documentation, the intent is to have the viewer treat this child as a representative child. The documentation presents the spirit of the nursery, the pedagogical principles at work, which may include one child as the protagonist here and another child as the protagonist there.

Documentation tries to raise questions about children's thinking and teaching strategies rather than mark the progress of all individual children. Documentation should always be defined in the context of at least the two other components, design and discourse. Technically, documentation is not an attempt to evaluate the effectiveness of teaching for all of the children. The viewer is asked to assume that what one sees in the documentation of one child has happened at other times with all of the children.

So it is in this chapter. Shihan represents all children in the nursery who are rich, resourceful and full of potential. Pedagogical documentation enables us to give visibility to this image of the child and to each child's uniqueness.

Glossary of terms

'Becoming' Where this is referred to in the book, it means that children can sometimes be seen as, for example, 'becoming' citizens rather than actually being in a real state of citizenship in the present.

Community of enquiry This term embraces the community involving parents and families, families and the community as well as children and educators.

Co-researchers/researchers Refers to an interpretation which is not academic; rather it is used in the sense that research is about 'finding out' about the world, life and living. It also is central to the Reggio Emilia approach and a documentation approach to early learning.

Culture of enquiry We used this term to describe a context where the ethos is characterised by support to be curious, to ask and pose questions and, hopefully, find solutions. This culture includes educators, children, parents and families.

Early years settings Refers to all those settings which care for and educate young children in the zero-to-five range.

Educators Refers to all professional staff working with young children in the early years settings.

Encounter This term is used here to describe the deep engagement of a person or persons in a discussion, dialogue, conversation or an episode or project.

Episode/project/long-term project All of these terms are explained quite specifically in Chapter 3.

Parents and families We have used these terms to include the extended family in the lives of children in relation to the early years setting. Using simply the term 'parents' or 'families' could have the effect of excluding one or the other.

Pedagogical Term used, in this context, to characterise the values, principles, cultural, social and political climate which underpins a documentation approach to early learning (Learning, Teaching Scotland 2005: 9).

Provocations/provocations for learning Refers to problems and challenges that can be presented by and to children to extend their learning within a particular interest, episode or project.

Reggio Emilia A municipality in northern Italy which has a worldwide reputation for its cutting-edge philosophy, thinking and practice with respect to early childhood education.

Bibliography

Boyd Cadwell, L. (2003) *Bringing Learning to Life: The Reggio Approach to Early Childhood Education*, New York and London: Teachers College Press.

Carr, M. (2001) *Assessment in Early Childhood Settings: Learning Stories*, London: Paul Chapman.

Clark, A. and Moss, P. (2001) *Listening to Young Children: The Mosaic Approach*, London and New York: National Children's Bureau for the Joseph Rowntree Foundation.

Clark, A., Kjorholt A.T. and Moss, P. (eds) (2005) *Beyond Listening*, Bristol: Policy Press.

Curtis, S.J. and Boultwood, M.E.A. (1963) *A Short History of Educational Ideas*, Cambridge: Cambridge University Press.

Dahlberg, G. (1999) 'Reflections on the Reggio Emilia Experience', in H. Penn (ed.) *Early Childhood Services* (chapter 11), Buckingham: Open University Press.

Dahlberg, G. and Moss, P. (2005) *Ethics and Politics in Early Childhood Education*, London and New York: Routledge Falmer.

Dahlberg, G., Moss, P. and Pence, A. (1999) *Beyond Quality in Early Childhood Education and Care, Post Modern Perspectives*, London: Falmer Press.

Donaldson, M. (1987) *Children's Minds*, London: Fontana Press.

Donaldson, M., Grieve, R. and Pratt, C. (eds) (1983) *Early Childhood Development and Education*, Oxford: Blackwell.

Dowling, M. (2000) *Young Children's Personal, Social and Emotional Development* (p. 68), London: Paul Chapman Publishing.

Edwards, C.P., Gandini, L. and Forman, G.E. (1998) *The Hundred Languages of Children, Advanced Reflections* (chapter 13), Norwood, NJ: Ablex Publishing Corporation.

Friere, P. (1972) *Pedagogy of the Oppressed*, London: Penguin Group.

Gandini, L. and Pope Edwards, C. (eds) (2001) *Bambini*, New York and London: Teachers College Press.

Greig, E. (2002) 'A Documentation Approach to Early Learning', Action Research Paper, Dundee University.

Greig, E. (2005) 'Impact of Dissemination Programme within Stirling Council Early Childhood Services', Action Research Paper, Dundee University.

Hallett, C. and Prout, A. (2003) *Hearing the Voices of Children: Social Policy for a New Century*, London: Routledge Falmer.

HMIE/Care Commission Report (2014) Education Scotland, Croftamie Nursery, Stirling, July.

Hull, K., Goldhaber, J. and Capone, A. (2001) *Opening Doors*, Boston, MA: Houghton Mifflin.

Lancaster, Y.P. (2003) *Listening to Young Children*, Maidenhead: Open University Press.

Lansdown, G. (2005) *Can You Hear Me? The Right of Young Children to Participate in Decisions Affecting Them*, The Hague: Bernard Van Leer Foundation.

Learning, Teaching Scotland (2005) *Let's Talk about Pedagogy*, Dundee: Learning, Teaching Scotland.

McLaren, P. and Leonard, P. (eds) (1993) *Paulo Freire: A Critical Encounter*, London: Routledge Falmer.

Malaguzzi, L. (2000) *The Hundred Languages of Children*, Italy: Reggio Children.

Meeuwig, M., Schepers, W. and van der Werf, T. (2009) *Traces from Reggio* (p. 79) Trude van Waarden.

Ministry of Education (1993) *Te Whariki*, Wellington: Learning Media.

Moss, P. and Petrie, P. (2002) *From Children's Services to Children's Spaces: Public Policy, Children and Childhood*, London: Routledge Falmer.

Pope Edwards, C., Gandini, L. and Forman, G. (1998) *The Hundred Languages of Children, the Reggio Emilia Approach – Advanced Reflections*, Greenwich, CT and London: Ablex.

Project Zero, Harvard Graduate School of Education and Reggio Children (2001) *Making Learning Visible: Children as Individuals and Group Learners*, Reggio Emilia: Reggio Children.

Rinaldi, C. (2001) *Making Learning Visible, Children as Individual and Group Learners* (p. 80), Italy: Project Zero, Reggio Children.

Rinaldi, C. (2002) 'An Audience with Carlina Rinaldi', MacRoberts Arts Centre, Stirling University, September.

Rinaldi, C. (2006) *In Dialogue with Reggio Emilia*, New York and London: Routledge.

Rogoff, B. (1990) *Apprenticeship in Thinking: Cognitive Development in Social Context*, New York: Oxford University Press.

Stirling Council (2001) *Children as Partners*, Stirling: Stirling Council Children's Services.

Stirling Council (2003) *Working with Documentation*, Stirling: Stirling Council Children's Services.

UNICEF (2006) *Implementing Child Rights in Early Childhood*, The Hague: Bernard Van Leer Foundation.

Whalley, P. (2001) *Involving Parents in their Children's Learning*, London: Paul Chapman.

Witherell, C. and Noddings, N. (1991) *Stories Lives Tell* (p. 280), New York: Teachers College Press.

Index

Bold page numbers indicate photographs.